POLICE, POLITICS, AND THE PRESS

Published by CopWorld Press

CopWorld Press
P.O. Box 3351
Ashland, OR 97520
email: sales@copworldpress.com

Cover & Interior Design: George Deyo

ISBN: 978-1-946754-15-8

Printed and Bound in the United States of America
First Edition 10 9 8 7 6 5 4 3 2 1

POLICE, POLITICS, AND THE PRESS

A FLORIDA CASE STUDY

HAVEN P. SIMMONS, Ph.D.
& PATRICK J. PROUDLER

COPWORLD PRESS ASHLAND, OREGON

Dedicated to my grandfather Haven Y. Simmons,
Uncle Bill Simmons, Luvy, and "Sunny" Simmons

CONTENTS

PROLOGUE

DUBIOUS HUMAN PROCLIVITIES exacerbated by systemic failings of government collide at the intersection of police, politics, and the press. With that being said, the authors never stop believing in the best intentions of respectable law enforcement officers who manifest the most positive aspects of this story. Aberrant police conduct is too often etched in the public mind and their daily sacrifices taken for granted, merely dismissed as being part of the job.

While the "Blue Code" saga escapes heavy publicity, it remains a notorious condemnation of police work. The opening chapter details a group of rogue officers, some of whom dodge retribution, if not detection. Others are punished and imprisoned. Political connections wield some influence in what transpires, a theme that gains momentum as the case study evolves.

The persuasion and public information chapter introduces the sheer force of elected officials, a reminder that the typical police officer is beholden to not only an immediate supervisor, but the administration and city hall. In essence, law enforcement agencies are an extension of the greater government expanse. In turn, public information officers and police personnel navigate a relationship with the press that hopefully builds the strongest possible reputation.

In crafting the cop narrative, the collaboration of public information officers with investigators and administrators is demonstrated through actual scenarios attracting media interest. But this narrative also relates to the internal machinations of policing that necessarily lead to actions and outcomes avoiding the public spotlight.

The sex crimes atrocity features an employee from a local newspaper obsessed with the mayor since he took office, igniting emotions that deflect from the police investigation. This toxic case garners national publicity, witnesses an incendiary throwdown between the publisher and public information officer representing the police department, and cements the paper's resolve to destroy the mayor and his minions at city hall.

The award-winning newspaper crusade in the public journalism chapter does not prevent construction of the Town Center entailing city hall and the police department proposed by the mayor, but proves to be his political downfall. An array of community factions, including the police union, coalesce around the relentless newspaper coverage to defeat the mayor's council supporters and diminish his power.

Submerged in media madness, police officers join two contentious camps, favoring the mayor and his opponent, the former executive editor of the newspaper, respectively. Emerging victorious, the journalist fulfills his pledge to initiate an autonomous internal affairs team to mitigate alleged indiscretions during his predecessor's reign. Unfortunately, political interference precipitates the new police chief's resignation, deposing of the senior investigator, eliminating the unit, and betraying editorials from his newspaper days extolling government trust, transparency, and accountability.

CHAPTER ONE

BREAKING THE BLUE CODE

GROWING UP IN Pennsylvania near Lake Erie, John Pradley and his childhood friends played many games, the most enjoyable of which was cops and robbers. Good guys and bad guys unfettered by the real-world nuances and influences in-between, conveying lessons in morality and decency that reflected the more pristine entertainment media portrayals of the era. Pradley somehow managed to assume the "good guy" role in most of the scenarios. After years of employment in the corporate world where profit margin was seemingly all that mattered, he fulfilled his childhood fantasy of becoming a police officer. The majority of officers he encountered in Brannon and Manson County served the citizens with courage and self-sacrifice, while others succumbed to temptations unbefitting of the profession.

Photographed by the *Tribune* standing beside his patrol car near a suspected drug den with the municipal police patch emblazoned on his sleeve and holding a shotgun, officer Bobby Haverkamp looked like anything but a rogue cop. The stocky Haverkamp, a six-year veteran on the department, had a commanding and self-assured presence, ostensibly inspiring confidence in the law-abiding citizens of the neighborhood.

Suspicions about Haverkamp, however, began after an elderly woman died of natural causes in her mobile home. Another patrol officer, Kelvin Hinrich, initially worked the case, completing all of the normal police functions: notifying the medical examiner and her relatives, securing the home and filing a report. Pradley was assigned as case detective to make sure no foul play occurred. He attended the autopsy and spoke to her son, who said he would be traveling from Michigan to claim the body.

Detective Pradley knew Haverkamp as a sullen bully, someone with a detached demeanor. Pradley met him for the first time when he finished the night shift and needed a ride to his house because the agency did not provide take-home vehicles. Haverkamp obliged, never saying a word as he drove the cruiser more than one hundred miles per hour along the main drag of First Avenue, and speeds exceeding seventy down residential streets to Pradley's house.

"You are out of your fucking mind. You can kill yourself if you want but don't endanger everybody else around," Pradley said as he nervously exited the vehicle.

Haverkamp laughed at him. "We're cops and we can act any way we want to. This is our city; people should look out for us."

Hinrich, in Pradley's mind, was the personification of a cop with the small man's complex. At five-foot-five, he was often abrupt and antagonistic with the public. He had probably never been in a fight, Pradley figured, and dearly deserved an ass kicking. He fancied himself god's gift to women, dressed the part, wore heavy cologne and neatly slicked back his black hair. He was also an incessant whiner.

One day after her death, a neighbor called police to report that the door to the mobile home was ajar. The responding officer determined that a burglary had taken place—the mobile home was ransacked and her car was missing.

Pradley informed her son of what had happened and they went to the mobile home. The son confirmed that much of his mother's jewelry was gone, along with her checkbook and credit cards. A month later, the son sent Pradley credit card bills reflecting numerous charges that were typically several hundred dollars at Brannon and nearby Sand Key stores. The car, meanwhile, was found abandoned near Manson County Beach.

Pradley followed up by interviewing a woman who delivered newspapers to the mobile home. She recalled seeing the door open at around 4:30 the morning the burglary occurred. She went to a nearby convenience store and told a police officer. She actually took him and a second officer to the mobile home and watched them make entry before continuing her route.

Interviews with area store clerks revealed that credit card purchases had been made by young white women. Customers fitting the same description also wrote checks on the elderly woman's account at grocery stores.

The burglary of the deceased woman's mobile home coincided with a veritable rash of "smash and grab" break-ins at jewelry stores, sporting goods outlets, computer stores and pawnshops. They invariably occurred in the early morning hours.

In addition, Pradley learned the deceased woman's telephone credit card had been used repeatedly over the phone on a state university campus one hundred miles away by a person identified as Bill Bromwell. He contacted Bromwell, who said the credit card number was given to him by Brannon resident James Stichcomb. Bromwell further alleged that Stinchcomb was known for selling stolen credit cards and making fraudulent purchases via computer and the postal service. Pradley arrested Bromwell for dealing in stolen property and use of a stolen credit card.

The case was unearthing some curious dimensions. On the day Bromwell was arrested, Haverkamp told a front desk officer at the police department that a friend, James Stichcomb, had asked him to find out what was going on with Pradley's investigation.

Haverkamp then confronted chief detective Wally Wallace, saying, "Pradley is going where he does not need to go in this case. Stinchcomb is a sick man who is on a lot of medication. Pradley is harassing him into making untrue statements. You should tell him to back off before he gets into trouble."

The following day, Wallace warned Pradley to "be careful" because Haverkamp was angry.

Bespectacled detective Ricardo Hillyard approached Pradley, explaining that he was concerned about activities at the Bay Breeze Apartments, a complex he had been living in and was about to become part-time manager of. According to Hillyard, Haverkamp and Stinchcomb were neighbors in the complex who sometimes carried computer and camera equipment to a vacant apartment and hung out together suspiciously in the late night and early morning hours. Hillyard also said he had seen a detailed map of a local golf shop in a storage shed at the complex. The shop was later burglarized. In Pradley's estimation, the detective possessed a remarkable reservoir of knowledge about the activities of Haverkamp and his associates.

One day, in the heat of an investigation, they chased a suspected bank robber in separate cars. After forcing the suspect to stop, they each exited their cruisers and surrounded his vehicle, Pradley on the driver's side and Hillyard on the passenger's. The suspect was armed, but in a frightening flash, Pradley realized he and Hillyard were looking more at each other than him. Pradley later imagined "Police officer killed in crossfire" as the newspaper headline pertaining to the story. While he and Hillyard affected the arrest and no one was hurt, the unsettling incident portended future danger and discontent.

Pradley located Stinchcomb at his Bay Breeze apartment. He was mostly uncooperative and extraordinarily nervous. He admitted to being involved in "computer billboard" work. He said Haverkamp was a close friend who advised him to tell Pradley absolutely nothing.

Pradley then asked Hillyard if he could meet with him and chief detective Wally Wallace to discuss the case further. It was possible he had additional information that only a police officer and resident of the apartment complex could provide. Hillyard agreed to the meeting, but only with his attorney present. He revealed that Haverkamp and Stinchcomb had met only minutes after Pradley departed the complex. In addition, he said there was probably much more to the case than met the eye but did not elaborate.

A few days later, both Haverkamp and Hinrich called the chief detective to complain about Pradley interviewing Stinchcomb. Just as before, Haverkamp claimed Stinchcomb was ill and labeled Pradley's actions harassment. Chief Vincent Ballentine, however, shut down the officers' demands to know particulars of the investigation.

Gyrating sensually to the music, Gina Kelser was a tall, leggy brunette with a body to die for. At least that was the consensus of Haverkamp and several other Brannon police officers who frequented a popular strip club called The Imagination. Haverkamp, in fact, was dating her at the time. People working the door, and even a few patrons, knew the revelers were cops. That was fine, too: being a cop didn't mean you couldn't party. Gina also had friends, good-looking college girls who seemed to love the uniform. It was exhilarating for the officers to have the power of arrest, influence, and sex appeal.

Apparently not all of Haverkamp's relationships with women, though, were going smoothly. His wife Cynthia called police regarding a domestic incident at their residence. She claimed her husband was abusive during a confrontation. No arrest was made because officers could not verify whether any violence occurred.

Given the incident involved one of his officers, Chief

Ballentine assigned Pradley to conduct an internal investigation. Haverkamp was flanked by patrol Sgt. Will Tovar during the interview and had little so say. Colleagues may accompany officers in the internal process to protect their rights. Haverkamp angrily dismissed the notion that he may have battered his wife. But he did try to convince Pradley that many cops abuse their wives because of stress on the job, a rationalization that failed to impress the detective.

Cynthia, meanwhile, alluded to rough treatment when questioned by Pradley about the allegation without being specific. In addition, she said her husband seemed to have more money than normal, and spoke of a ring he had given the wife of a friend as a birthday present. The friend, as it turned out, was Sgt. Tovar.

The sandy-haired Tovar walked with a slight limp and always seemed to move his shoulder nervously. He had survived a fatal shootout with a deranged gunman. He was known as a tough and somewhat controversial cop. Only in his thirties, he was arguably the closest friend of Mayor Evans on the entire police force. Tovar was seen frequently in Evans's office; he was an excellent source of inside information about what was going on in the department. He had even been invited to social functions at Evans's home, a distinction very few Brannon police officers could claim.

When Evans and public information officer Hank Siebert were threatened by a lunatic angry about alleged code violations at his girlfriend's home, it was Tovar who paid the man a visit. It was one thing to menace receptionists and other city hall employees; his ire toward the mayor and Siebert was another. Chief detective Wallace learned he had recently been released from the state penitentiary. Even scarier, his rap sheet included convictions for arson and criminal mischief against a government building. Tovar confronted him at his home, saying he knew who his parole officer was and one false move against the mayor or Siebert would get him kicked out of town and sent back to the clink. The ex-con later called Siebert to ask why this lieutenant was hounding him. Siebert pleaded ignorance, and never heard from him again.

Suspicious there could be a connection to the burglaries, Pradley convinced Tovar to relinquish the ring his wife had received from Haverkamp. Sure enough, the owner of a local jewelry store confirmed the ring had been stolen in a recent burglary. Tovar noted that a friend had told him Haverkamp was involved in some area burglaries. According to Tovar, the friend also mentioned Hinrich and another officer, Jim McManus, in connection with break-ins. A sickening, awkward feeling descended upon Pradley: he was a cop investigating cops, but any disgust or affinity he might feel for fellow officers must be tempered by meeting his obligation to pursue the case.

Pradley determined that Haverkamp and the muscular, pock-marked McManus coached a local Little League team together. They furnished the players with a dozen pairs of socks stolen in the burglary of the sporting goods store. Haverkamp and McManus befriended another coach and owner of an auction house in Manson County, Albert Adler. The two of them, along with Tovar, were hired as security guards at Adler's warehouses. Pradley found that a couple of warehouses had been burglarized and some items stolen before Adler decided to part ways with the officers.

Because the alleged crimes occurred in the county and the suspicious Adler was apparently reluctant to press charges himself, Pradley asked sheriff's detectives to investigate. They never did. The mayor, he surmised, learned of the allegations from his children who worked as deputies for Sheriff Chas Wellman. Further, it was possible the mayor asked the man he was instrumental in getting elected or another supervisor at the sheriff's office to abandon the case tormenting the Brannon police.

Pradley spent hours tracking receipts from other checks and credit cards stolen during the burglaries to nearby Tallemay Bay. Realizing the scope of the case, he then contacted state investigators who linked the credit card transactions to a drug and prostitution ring in Tallemay Bay.

The police department building was ramshackle, to put it mildly. It was nearly fifty years old. The paint was peeling, storage and filing space was at a premium, and important conversations with suspects could be heard by virtually anyone walking down the foreboding corridors. The cramped, squalid shift rooms contained torn, coffee-stained couches. Most officers regarded Evans's assurances that a new facility would be built as mere lip service, especially those resenting his purported unwillingness to fund new cars and equipment.

One of them was Detective Jimmy Spangler, a meticulous individual who shared a tiny office with Pradley and sprayed disinfectant on his desk each day at ten minutes before five o'clock prior to leaving for home. They were not social friends, but Spangler and Pradley had worked closely on a number of crucial cases through the years, both providing important information to Siebert about investigations and participating in "perp walks" to garner publicity. Spangler and his wife, meanwhile, were raising a daughter and struggling to make ends meet on the perceived pittance provided by the city. He contemptuously called the mayor "fat boy" and numerous expletives for not approving high enough raises. Being a police officer, however, was his ultimate dream; it was the only career he had ever desired, and detective work made it even sweeter. He seemingly moved from a crouch with hunched shoulders, his protruding chin and no-nonsense demeanor personifying the image of a cop on the trail of the bad guys.

Will Tovar, though, was not one of the mayor's detractors. Following a meeting with Evans, the chief informed Pradley that Tovar would be working jointly with him on the Haverkamp case. The sergeant suddenly donned street clothes instead of his dark blue police uniform. Some people may have wondered about Tovar's assignment, but no one asked questions: if Evans wanted him to investigate, so be it.

Pradley forged ahead, interviewing several of the young women, a couple of whom shacked up on a regular basis at Bay Breeze. They referred to a prominent Brannon businessman and computer store owner who enjoyed hanging around police officers. Isaac Casper liked to "ride along" with officers in the evening. The officers included Tovar, McManus and Haverkamp, the three primary members of the department's elite tactical squad. Casper, an obvious wannabe cop, was certified by Tovar to carry the PR24 nightstick of Rodney King infamy, and did so almost constantly with the police administration's blessing.

Casper was also willing to "ride along" with Pradley to various locations that the burglaries occurred. The panicked Casper said several police officers would "cover" for each other by committing the burglaries and writing the reports as the investigating officers. McManus, he said, served as a lookout for Haverkamp. He later took Pradley and Tovar to his residence, displaying a computer monitor allegedly taken during a burglary committed by himself and Haverkamp. He added that stolen property was exchanged with accomplices in Tallemay Bay for credit cards. In the burglary of a luggage store, he said, he and Haverkamp damaged the rear door to make it appear there was forced entry. In fact, they had obtained a key from an employee they knew at the store. According to McManus, some of the luggage was turned over to Hillyard, who gave it to a female acquaintance to "shut her up" about an incident that had occurred between them at the Brannon Holiday Inn.

Indeed, one of Pradley's sources claimed Haverkamp and Hillyard each had affairs with two of the young "groupies" who followed the officers around. One of the women, Marti Fletcher, apparently fabricated a stolen check and credit card scheme at Haverkamp's behest. Hinrich wrote the report about the alleged thefts from her car. Fletcher, according to Pradley and Tovar, purchased televisions, cameras, clothing and food on checks and credit cards that were not actually stolen. Her brother, Wayne, was a Brannon police officer not directly implicated in the case. The second woman, Jan

Horner, told Pradley that Haverkamp also kept narcotics seized in drug arrests rather than turn them over to the department for evidence.

Partying at the Bay Breeze swimming pool with the young women was commonplace for the officers. Drinks were plentiful the night McManus, Hillyard, Wayne Fletcher and some friends decided to go swimming. Unfortunately, Fletcher and one of the revelers, Mark Patterson, got into a fistfight. In a familiar pattern, Patterson was arrested and later reported his credit card missing.

With the investigation heating up, Haverkamp called Tovar at his home asking "what he had to confess to." Haverkamp conceded a confession could be in order, but that his role in the crimes had been exaggerated. Computer geek Stinchcomb, meanwhile, notified police that Haverkamp threatened to "kill" him if any officers got into trouble because of his comments to investigators.

Shaken by the experience, Casper attempted suicide by overdosing on medicine at his computer office. He left a note explaining how his property should be divided. He survived following treatment at Manson Memorial Hospital and was then admitted for psychiatric observation.

One of the young females wasn't as fortunate. Sarah Dane died in a jet ski crash on the Cedar River only days earlier. Haverkamp and McManus were present when the tragedy occurred. They reported it to the Manson Sheriff's Office, which had jurisdiction over the investigation and ruled it an accident. There was no mention of foul play.

The investigation also implicated Brannon police Sgt. Doug Maxwell, who allegedly stored numerous police radios at his home that were not assigned to him. Pradley determined the radios were used by the suspects in the crime spree. Maxwell resigned abruptly from the force.

Meanwhile, a burglary report was sent back from the Brannon police records section indicating there weren't enough serial numbers reference a pistol stolen from a pawnshop. When Pradley questioned Hinrich, the officer who filed the report, he became agitated and refused to speak. Pradley started following him after work. On several occasions, Hinrich would go to the storage shed at the Bay Breeze apartment complex.

Based on their suspicions, Pradley and an agent from the Florida Department of Law Enforcement executed a search warrant on the shed, locating burglar tools, a dark jump suit previously described as one worn by Haverkamp during the break-ins, and other incriminating items including stolen merchandise.

Pradley was attempting to relax at home one evening when the phone rang. It was Hinrich. He complained about the investigation, saying it was heavy-handed and unfair. Pradley refused to dignify the remarks, other than explaining that he was not at liberty to discuss the case unless Hinrich were willing to give a formal, taped statement. Pradley also suggested that he could talk to Chief Ballentine. Hinrich slammed down the phone.

But Ballentine was, in reality, of limited utility. Pradley had personally requested help from the Florida Department of Law Enforcement (FDLE) after Ballentine, sending mixed messages about the veracity of the department's willingness to fully expose the case, refused to read a fifteen-page summation of the suspicious activities and criminal conduct, tossing it derisively on his desk.

According to Pradley, "When the cops are the bad guys, it is a whole different story. They know you are out to nail them, and the only way you will is to have solid, tangible evidence up front. Deny, deny, deny is the officers' motto. They know that they can intimidate witnesses and have other cops lie for them. Confessions almost never happen, but disclosure will if they sense there is no way out."

Pradley was in the unenviable position of investigating officers in a department without a formal internal affairs unit. His findings could be rebuffed and resented by police administrators and the mayor himself. "If an officer committed what might seem to be a criminal offense, the police administration assigned a general case detective to investigate, guiding his investigation and report writing, often resulting in the officer's acquittal and a mayoral thumbs up," he explained.

The gravity of the Havercamp case and role of FDLE, however, meant someone would necessarily be held accountable as Pradley traversed a perilous tightrope in his own agency.

Tovar alleged he was receiving anonymous death threats at his house. In fact, a patrol officer reported that Hinrich had told him someone should "do" Tovar, i.e. shoot him.

The situation worsened the evening Pradley's teenaged son was followed in his car and run off the road by someone driving a green Chevy Blazer. Despite the harrowing experience, the boy was able to get the license tag of the vehicle and return home unharmed. Pradley was not only angry, but worried. Now his family was at risk. He first called the

Brannon police, who matched the tag with Hinrich's vehicle. He next contacted the state police, three of whom showed up at his house within an hour. Based on Pradley's statements, they staked out Hinrich's residence and swiftly converged on the suspect as he drove into the driveway early the next morning. Pradley watched appreciatively as Hinrich was handcuffed and placed in the back seat of the police car. They charged him with numerous felonies in connection with the burglaries.

To say Pradley celebrated Hinrich's arrest was an understatement. Their differences had become very nasty before the incident with Pradley's son. Pradley had heard from several officers that Hinrich was calling him a "snitch" at the department. One night during late shift matters came to a head in the parking lot.

"I don't appreciate what you've been saying about me. You've been telling people I can't be trusted."

"You are going to get hurt if you keep acting this way, Pradley."

"I'm doing my goddam job, which is more than you can say."

"Keep talking and see where it gets you."

"You are a piece of shit," Pradley said as he pushed the younger officer out of the way.

Hinrich went back inside the building and, as he had on countless occasions throughout the case, Pradley recognized just how difficult it was to be a cop under those conditions.

Several of the young women and Stinchcomb were arrested shortly thereafter.

Pradley obtained an arrest warrant and started looking

for Haverkamp, and he was nowhere to be found. Getting the warrant to arrest a cop had not been easy, but the judge agreed because of the mounting evidence. A few days later, an article appeared in the *Herald* quoting Haverkamp as saying that a Brannon police detective was going to kill him. Haverkamp was nearly portrayed as the victim in the piece, and brokered a deal through the newspaper to turn himself in to Sheriff Wellman in the middle of the Tallemay Bay Bridge, thirty miles north of Brannon.

Several media outlets photographed Wellman arresting Haverkamp, who claimed he needed to be out of range should Pradley opt to shoot him. One headline from the *Tribune* read "Ex-officer's badge seen as crime lure." The *Tallemay Times*, demonstrating neutrality and objectivity as a regional rather than local newspaper, ran an extensive story that concluded the officers used their knowledge of criminal investigations to remain undetected for more than a year.

The relieved Pradley learned that Haverkamp had called other officers at the department on several occasions seeking details about the warrant, wanting to know what he "had to give up" in hopes of cutting a deal with police and prosecutors. After his arrest, he declined interviews with Pradley, communicating through his attorney.

Haverkamp was ultimately charged with sixty-one crimes. Like the media, state prosecutors focused heavily on Haverkamp as the ringleader. He served three years behind bars and became a tree trimmer in Brannon upon his release. Despite newfound freedom, he said the stress of the case precluded him from speaking. His only mode of communication was writing notes. He later returned to prison for possession of firearms as a convicted felon. After two years in prison, Hinrich moved to a remote part of the state, where he was under surveillance for allegedly cultivating marijuana. McManus left the department and was not prosecuted. He managed a gun range in Brannon and supposedly got hooked on crack cocaine. Hillyard and Tovar were not charged, achieving higher rank in the agency over the years.

Siebert was hired as Public Information Officer (PIO) just as the Haverkamp case concluded. Local media coverage failed to capture the depth of the atrocities and the number of officers implicated even though the investigative documents were public record, readily available to reporters. Conspiracy theorists contended there were deeper, darker connections with ramifications for the greater community. The *Brannon Herald* and *Sabella Tribune* rarely squandered opportunities to embarrass the mayor, the city, and the Brannon Police Department (BPD). Official statements embracing the generic "it is an ongoing investigation" from police administrators were presumably guided by the mayor. It is feasible the regular interaction of Siebert and reporters would have altered media involvement to a degree.

Indeed, Siebert's role with the police department grew gradually as high-profile cases intensified media interest. In time, he and Pradley developed implicit rapport and confidentiality that brought the agency out of the shadows by generating greater publicity. Detectives, after all, typically investigate the most heinous and intriguing felonies following initial response by the patrol division.

CHAPTER TWO

PERSUASION AND PUBLIC INFORMATION

"**I HATE WILSON** Evans and Hank Siebert."

Those words, according to Dan Brody, public information officer for the sheriff's office, were uttered by a city editor for the *Tribune* as he was being transferred to another office. The PIO reminded him that Siebert answered to the mayor, not the paper. Brody was supportive of Siebert because they became friends working together as television reporters covering city hall and Chas Wellman's campaign for sheriff. They were considered civilian public information officers with commercial media backgrounds, then the trendy pick among law enforcement agencies in the area. Wellman believed it was best to enlist a PIO who understood the mindset of reporters and would adapt to the laws, policies, and machinations of police culture. Conversely, the advantage of sworn personnel in the role was intimate familiarity with law enforcement and the credence of wearing the uniform during media interviews. Some larger agencies enjoy the luxury of employing PIOs from both backgrounds to balance the pendulum.

Unlike so many people who escape the north in their elderly years, Siebert relocated as a twenty-four-year-old from Iowa, certain of being a sports writer his entire life. The only reporting job available at a daily newspaper in Sabella, due south of Brannon, was as a police reporter. It was a tremendous learning experience for Siebert, who worked the cop beat eight hours a day making contacts, some of whom would become good friends despite the supposed affront to journalistic detachment. He wrote everything from police briefs, to features like one on a motorcycle cop, hard news and accident stories. He also covered courts and trials. He learned to perceive most police officers as fundamentally dedicated and honest. His boss, the managing editor, eschewed compliments, was hard-nosed, and taught Siebert to be fearful and respect authority over two-point-five years on the job. When he decided to leave the Sabella paper, Siebert applied at the *Brannon Herald*, interviewing with one of the editors, Warren Posley, who told him he was not a good fit in the "culture" of Manson County. Soon thereafter, thanks to an enthusiastic reference by the chief detective of the Sabella Sheriff's Office, he became the Manson County reporter for the ABC television affiliate in the area, where his comprehension of government, law enforcement and the bigger picture grew appreciably. Little did he know that the initial police reporting job would lead him to television and public relations, including the position with Mayor Evans and the Brannon police.

As PIO, Siebert knew Evans really alienated the *Tribune* not long before his landslide re-election to a fifth term. He was upset that the newspaper's editorial board had refused to endorse him. His victory celebration at a downtown waterfront hotel was covered by all of the local media. But, when it was discovered a reporter and photographer from the *Tribune* were on the premises, he had them escorted out of the party by a hulking off-duty police officer. The following morning, the mayor and his city grants writer stood in front of the newspaper building holding signs thanking voters for their support.

In addition, he told Siebert not to release any information to the *Tribune* unless it was required under state public records laws. So, after making general statements at the police department to the media about a case involving alleged improprieties by the city clerk, Siebert addressed questions from every reporter except the one from the *Tribune*. Siebert simply advised him to check the police reports and that he had nothing further to say. It wasn't a comfortable situation for Siebert or the reporter, but he honored the mayor's wishes.

The *Tribune* had apparently joined the *Herald's* crusade against the mayor and anyone loosely associated with him. One of their editorials, titled "Brannon's bully mayor," excoriated Siebert for adhering to Evans's new policy. They poked fun at Evans for pouting, but conceded that it was his party and he could cry if he wanted to, in the spirit of Lesley Gore's smash oldies song.

The editorial continued, "When Evans's petty and mean-spirited attitude is imposed or adopted by city employees, it's clear the mayor has gone too far with his practice of retribution against anyone who dares to challenge him."

There was probably some irony in the mayor's turmoil with the local newspapers. He had groomed Chas Wellman to be sheriff after hiring him as Brannon police chief following a scandal over officers stealing narcotics from the department's evidence room. With the mayor's political support, the ruggedly handsome Wellman was narrowly elected sheriff, parlaying his charisma into a veritable love affair with the media. His innovations, including juvenile boot camps and a program to combat early release of violent criminals from prison, earned him two appearances on *60 Minutes* and national acclaim. His relationship with the local media, cultivated initially during two years as chief, also hastened county and state approval of generous annual budget increases. The mayor's troubles with the newspapers, meanwhile, always seemed to place the city under the sort of media microscope most elected officials dread to the core.

An ex-state trooper and investigator for the state prosecutor's office, Wellman was credited, at least publicly, for cleaning up the municipal police department and helping the volatile Evans quell union sympathizers in the agency. He had agreed to become chief with the understanding that Evans, himself a former cop, would not meddle in his administration. For the most part, Evans kept his word. Wellman became sheriff at only forty, outgrowing his fun-loving persona to build a regime lasting over two decades. Word around Brannon was that the county commission would buy the sheriff fighter jets and tanks if he requested them in the name of curtailing crime.

Evans replaced Wellman with Ballentine, who had left his job as a state trooper in New York to become a parking ticket officer with the Brannon police. Indeed, doubling as police commissioner and mayor, the powerful Evans ensured the city council would appoint the police chiefs he recommended. Ballentine's quantum leap to police chief turned heads and alienated some of the agency's top brass, but he had endeared himself to Evans on a personal level. The mayor liked Ballentine's energy and enthusiasm for assuming the job in private conversations, traits that surfaced sporadically once he became chief. Evans was generally disappointed in Ballentine's performance despite his evident willingness to take direction for nearly a decade.

A content analysis of editorials over eight years portraying the mayor and Sheriff Wellman confirmed the newspaper's apparent obsession with Evans and "his" city, including the police department. During that time period, thirty-four of seventy-one opinion pieces about the mayor were categorized as negative, while the sheriff gleaned positive depictions in thirteen of twenty-seven editorials. Positive ratings were attributed to commending, applauding, approving or admiring editorials; negative ratings embodied faulting, blaming, censuring or disapproving ones.

In stark contrast to Mayor Evans, Sheriff Wellman was consistently lauded for his accountability, fiscal platforms, and leadership qualities.

Evans was pilloried for refusing to spend any of the city's $27 million reserve on the Police Athletic League, relinquishing it to the Manson County Sheriff's Office. The sheriff's humanity was championed for upgrading educational programs at PAL: "He (the sheriff) was a dropout himself—a fact that still brings tears to his eyes."

The mayor was described as "indifferent" when a police officer fatality shot an alleged drug dealer: "No words of reassurance have come from city hall, no expression of sympathy" for the bereaved family.

If the sheriff made such statements in the aftermath of a civilian traffic fatality, they were not mentioned editorially. The accident was conceivably caused by deputies who were chasing a criminal suspect, but the newspapers endorsed the agency's policy on pursuits.

The mayor's fiscal philosophy was impugned editorially when the newspaper called for a referendum to build a new public safety complex, alleging the city was "seriously falling behind in such basic service as police and fire protection" owing to "12 years of the no-new-taxes administration." But several years later, Mayor Evans's proposal to construct a public safety complex called the "Town Center" faced a groundswell of opposition instigated by the *Herald*.

The *Herald* assailed the mayor for "union busting" at the city's fire department, "just as he broke the police union, in the process destroying several veteran officers' careers and crippling the department."

"I write what the editorial board wants to stand for—the paper's position; it's up to me to create a readable piece and make the choice of words." said the *Herald's* chief editorial writer, Daniel Klemmert, in assessing the depictions of the mayor and sheriff. "The mayor is much too thin-skinned. He lets criticism color his views of policy and opponents. The sheriff started out with a thin skin (when he was hired by the mayor at the police department) but he has learned to control his temper and how to handle criticism."

He named "fairness, balance and truthfulness" as his espoused journalistic standards.

"The media want to run the government," lamented the mayor. "This newspaper tries to run it through editorials." He called Klemmert a "yellow journalist who never had a very good attitude about me. When you proved him wrong on something, he wouldn't put it in or make a correction."

The mayor also said that complaints about Klemmert's virulence were largely unheeded by the publisher and executive editor, Warren Posley. The relationship disintegrated in social and community venues, where the mayor sometimes lambasted the paper. Hard feelings were inflamed by the mayor's letters to the editor and his messages to residents in the city newsletter.

Editorials invariably concentrated more on the mayor's style and comportment than his actual policies: "Politicians can be expected to use the course of events to their political advantage. But, with Evans, treating the office as his office is pervasive, and in our view, unhealthy."

Another study examined the relationship of officers from the Brannon Police Department, Manson County Sheriff's Office, Sabella Police Department, and Sabella Sheriff's Office with reporters and media organizations that covered the agencies on a regular basis. A high percentage of officers responded to questionnaires, some of which inspired follow up personal interviews with the researcher, who allowed participants to remain anonymous.

The first pattern of perception among respondents entailed closing ranks (forty-eight law enforcement officers and one veteran radio reporter) who frequently chastised the tactics and motives of reporters, while harboring greater respect for their own profession and contemporaries. Brannon police were more prevalent in the group than Manson sheriff's personnel, although the neighboring Sabella County Sheriff's Office dominated the pattern.

According to a Brannon police administrator concerning the *Herald*, "We're not dealing with rocket scientists here. I've met with editors to resolve our problems, but it doesn't trickle down to the reporters. Of course, they've been after the mayor for a long time. I prefer dealing with the broadcast media. When you go on camera, when you say something, that's what you hear on television."

The closing ranks officers agreed that reporters rarely portray law enforcement officers in a positive light, and that matters of deployment, detection, budget, and internal affairs should not be divulged.

"One reason why we sometimes say nothing is because of fear that a hungry reporter will make accusations toward the officer and he and his family will suffer. Before a reporter degrades an officer maybe they need to look at themselves," commented a police patrolman.

Another Brannon police administrator added, "Our operational people don't always have the time or patience to deal with reporters. And the reporters don't cultivate sources and develop personal relationships as much these days. Maybe economics has something to do with it. We would have a more adversarial relationship with the media without the PIO."

The second pattern, watchdogs asserting the media are responsible for challenging the status quo and closely scrutinizing the actions of government to protect the public interest, consisted of nine newspaper reporters and seven television reporters.

A *Tribune* reporter stated: "I believe the media best serves the public by being a true 'watchdog' of all government agencies, including law enforcement. That philosophy requires a large dose of skepticism and thus spawns an adversarial relationship. Goals of the media and law enforcement often clash. Wise cops and reporters understand their differences and learn to work together despite them. The less-educated, less-experienced cops create problems. Some less intelligent cops think they can't tell you anything."

A watchdog television reporter conceded, "I have gained more respect for law enforcement than I had when I started reporting. A lot of reporters don't have that respect. The police have a tough job. The criminal has more constitutional rights than the police."

Watchdogs believed that too many law enforcement officers tended to label them as crime-thirsty ghouls, and disagreed with allegations that they often sensationalized stories to boost circulation and ratings.

A *Herald* editor admitted newspapers also suffered from time and staffing constraints: "To me, having more of a rotating beat system reflects how coverage of the whole community has expanded. Now we have reporters looking for stories on social issues—daycare and the like. Cop reporters are asked to do other things. It's a professional, business relationship, and we have the freedom to go after what we want to. On the down side, we've lost tips. Too often our mistake is attacking the cop beat from the one source, the public information officer."

Twenty-five law enforcement officers and six broadcast reporters comprised conciliation, the third pattern of perception. Ten of the officers were from the Manson County Sheriff's Office, perhaps reflecting Chas Wellman's purportedly proactive approach to media relations.

Conciliation respondents were much more adamant than the other groups that a cooperative media-law enforcement relationship provides the public with more valuable information than an adversarial one.

According to a Manson sheriff's administrator, "We work for the public. They should be informed. We need to keep an open dialogue with the community because we are constitutionally required to keep citizens informed. It's called being above board. Most law enforcement officers who have not been in a management role do not understand the value of the media."

In the opinion of conciliation respondents, media frequently assist law enforcement by publishing information on missing children and wanted criminals, and that cooperative reporters are rewarded with the most substantive information about crime and law enforcement, a reciprocal arrangement especially important to detectives investigating major cases.

"I believe most police officers really care about what they are doing. The crime rate is high and they have a tough job to do. I don't harp on them and I don't assume the worst," a Sabella television reporter said.

The conciliation group endorsed the idea that public information officers were more interested in providing reporters with useful information than promoting the police chief or sheriff. They contended that PIOs did a good job of directing reporters to knowledgeable sources in law enforcement agencies, providing punctual feedback, and convening press conferences.

A television reporter stated: "We have deadlines for stories. We want the information as quickly as possible and most PIOs in law enforcement understand this need. There are also a couple of PIOs who arrange 'walks' of criminal suspects. It's great video."

"The PIO can convey information to the public more accurately. It fosters a good relationship between the press, the police, and the public. The PIO is really a relief during major incidents, when detectives are tied up on their cases," added a Brannon police administrator.

Media depictions of politicians and law enforcement strongly influence the public information function that juggles the responsibility for being above board with protecting police intelligence and sensitive investigations. On that basis, Siebert's role at the Brannon Police Department was increasingly pivotal.

CHAPTER THREE

CRAFTING THE COP NARRATIVE

BRANNON IS HOME to a major citrus company and regional headquarters for a national sporting goods chain. Downtown Brannon is mostly government buildings. But U.S. 61 is a congested north-south corridor through Brannon with endless restaurants and bars serving the most important contributors to the local economy: tourists. Ocean and bay-front properties are exorbitantly expensive, usually purchased by wealthy retirees with deep pockets. Sunbathers blanket beautiful white sand beaches lined with palm trees, condominiums and motels.

The desirable areas of Brannon and Manson County bear little resemblance to the community's lower east side inhabited mostly by blacks and Hispanics. In fact, the visitors and well-heeled segments of the population have probably never seen the modest homes and decaying apartment complexes, many of which were constructed decades ago with federal subsidies. There is little relief from the ceaseless heat for those who cannot afford air conditioners.

Corporal A.J. Henderson had been with the force four years the night he received a call on the eastside about a landlord-tenant altercation. Due in part to the mayor's frugality, the Brannon Police Department had fewer sworn officers than most agencies of equivalent size, so they rarely worked in pairs. It was another infernal summer evening as Henderson rolled up on the apartment complex alone in his blue Ford Crown Victoria.

What happened after that is a matter of conjecture. According to Henderson, he observed the landlord arguing outside with a black male about rent he allegedly had not paid. As he walked toward the men, Henderson said, the tenant started to run away. A foot pursuit ensued through yards and over fences. At one point, the barefooted tenant with dreadlocks grabbed a shovel and hurled it at the officer before resuming his sprint. Both were bandy-legged when the suspect turned around to confront the officer with a broken bottle he found on the ground. Henderson said warnings to drop the bottle were ignored and, when the man began approaching him aggressively, he did what recruits are taught in the law enforcement academy: discharge the firearm until the individual no longer poses a threat. Three bullets from the service revolver found their mark, and the tenant dropped dead on the ground.

Ensuing interviews revealed the man was a volatile illegal alien from Haiti who had threatened family members with a knife in the past, but for now many neighbors were enraged at the officer. Within minutes, dozens of people converged on the scene, many of them convinced it was yet another example of a white cop offing an innocent black civilian. The crowd ultimately swelled to nearly two hundred people. Henderson felt the combination of fear and adrenaline when he shot Pedro Porre; now he felt the wrath of bystanders, two of whom would later tell the media and investigators Porre was gunned down in cold blood. They claimed Henderson fired as Porre turned and ran away.

Fortunately, an officer provided Henderson with backup, emerging from his cruiser with one of the department's police dogs. The K-9 and two officers stood their ground as paramedics and more police were dispatched to the scene. About a dozen Brannon police officers were soon joined by twenty sheriff's deputies and a few state troopers. Among other things, they had to cordon off several blocks around the area. The gravity of the situation was obvious as residents screamed at the "killer cops" and implored them to leave. Police and state's attorney investigators canvassed the neighborhood, even going door to door for witnesses in an effort to gain some consensus about what happened. It was a miracle that no one else was injured or killed during the five-hour ordeal. In addition, the shooting received no immediate media coverage because it occurred past the newspaper deadlines for the next morning and the late evening television news.

Pradley tried to comfort Henderson, hustling him into a cruiser and returning to the police station for his own reflection and protection. The shaken officer was placed on administrative leave and relieved of his firearm. Henderson would hole up in his apartment for weeks, receiving solace from Pradley and several other officers who offered him their guns because his life could be at risk.

Mayor Evans's office was abuzz the following morning. The mayor had learned that hundreds of eastside residents were attending a rally at noon to protest the shooting. It was sure to attract a throng of media. A white cop-black civilian shooting was enough to fray nerves and exacerbate a tenuous relationship between the municipal police and local African-American residents. Historically, escalated police presence in east Brannon prompted accusations of harassment. A more passive presence, meanwhile, spurred claims the police and elected officials did not care about the neighborhood; that residents were left helplessly at the mercy of drug dealers and the criminal element. It was the "damned if you do, damned if you don't" law enforcement dynamic fostering tension in many cities.

The mayor quickly phoned a couple of elderly women in the neighborhood, long-time political allies who might help diffuse the more contentious emotions at the rally. He also instructed his new police chief, David Thayer, not to attend. Any visible police presence, the mayor ascertained, would likely aggravate emotions. The buck stopped with Mayor Evans, and he would be accountable for what was happening in the city. Not only that: per city charter, he was police commissioner of the city, a former cop who took a stern but personal interest in the department.

The mayor decided that he, grants writer Jerry Walz, and Siebert should attend the rally. Siebert, in his opinion, could placate the various Tallemay Bay media who might be there. Walz was arguably his most beloved and devoted employee, the fellow who secured a $1 million federal Drug Free Communities grant and provided even more inside information about sentiments and people in city government than Sgt. Will Tovar. Every morning, Evans and Walz would hold an informal meeting with the mayor's secretary of nearly twenty years, Jenny Bowles, to discuss the latest city scuttlebutt. City employees understood that the middle-aged, slippery Walz was the mayor's eyes and ears, a direct conduit to the second floor of city hall. He would scurry down the hallway screaming for the mayor in his signature high-pitched voice. Other regular insiders in the mayor's office were: the impeccably dressed and groomed city clerk, Clark Kelley, the sheriff's brother-in-law; public works director Ed Courtley, a deceptively smart and gentlemanly Florida native who understood the mayor and was discreetly faithful; and, depending upon the circumstances, Siebert, and the chief of police, sometimes with Tovar in tow.

Several patrol officers in cruisers were within seconds of the little strip mall where the rally was held just in case there was trouble. Emotions at the rally ran the gamut from relatively calm to livid. A pocket of especially angry young to middle-aged males descended on the mayor for explanations. He informed them the case was under investigation and that Cpl. Henderson had been placed on administrative leave. He also conveyed his condolences to friends and family of Porre.

One of the angriest men told the mayor his comments were insincere; that something must be done to ebb the unconscionable attacks by racist police officers against blacks. He also accused the mayor of losing control of his city and its police force. Evans nearly busted a gasket, and the two escalated into a screaming match. The mayor deduced his adversary was actually from Sabella, not Brannon. Standing only inches from each other, the three-hundred-pound Evans instructed the man to go back where he came from and keep his nose out of Brannon's affairs.

Siebert made certain the mayor granted interviews to several reporters. The idea was to balance the publicity spectrum, since some residents of the rally claimed Henderson committed cold-blooded murder. The mayor's good relationship with area television stations paid off: newscasts that evening treated the story equitably. The *Herald*, meanwhile, editorially urged the city and state department of law enforcement to investigate the shooting thoroughly in the interest of resolution and racial harmony.

David Thayer was handpicked by Evans to succeed Ballentine, the somewhat reclusive police chief seemingly eager to collect his second retirement. From the instant Thayer assumed the role, he applied more proactive media and community relations tactics than his predecessor. But like Siebert, he would suffer some "guilt by association" at the local newspapers for his affiliation with Evans. Thayer had worked his way through the agency, beginning as a patrol officer in his late teens. At forty-one, he was a relatively young police chief. The father of four daughters and a devout Christian, Thayer was fairly short with forearms like a blacksmith. He could show a sensitive side, interspersed with the sort of coarse humor heard frequently in the police culture. He was also grateful and devoted to the mayor because of his appointment to the position.

Thayer breathed a sigh of relief the day he received the state department of law enforcement report on the Porre shooting. Cpl. Henderson had been exonerated by the agency, which ostensibly provided a detached, unbiased perspective on what occurred that night. It mirrored the findings of the Brannon department's internal investigation, something that Siebert conveyed to the media with pleasure in a press release. It also helped the city rebound from adverse publicity of a march from the east end, past the police department and city hall to remember Porre and protest the shootings. It did not, however, pacify African-American residents, including the president of the local NAACP (National Association for the Advancement of Colored People). To them, it was little more than a murder cover-up orchestrated by law enforcement.

The *Tallemay Bay Times*, in fact, ran a lengthy story revisiting the shooting and past problems between the Brannon police and African-American residents, including Tovar's fatal shootout with a suspected drug dealer. Thayer was interviewed for the article, saying he was doing his best to mend fences by holding meetings with residents and instituting more community policing strategies in east Brannon. In the article, Thayer championed the Drug Free Communities Weed and Seed program, which meant weeding out criminals from neighborhoods and planting the seeds of prosperity. Government subsidies were supposedly provided to entice local entrepreneurship, along with drug education and a joint narcotics task force. Thayer and several officers held a cookout not long after the shooting, playing basketball and mingling with African-American eastside residents. The reporter also interviewed several disgruntled black residents. One, a retired school board member, likened the shooting to police misconduct in the O.J. Simpson case.

Chief Thayer started the "Chief Is In" program to thaw relations with the law-abiding eastside residents and send a message to the intimidating local crack dealers. It also garnered him, the department and the city some excellent publicity. At Siebert's urging, the two local newspapers and most of the regional television stations followed the chief mid-morning to a street corner notorious for drug transactions. Flanked by Tovar and Capt. Tom Miller, the miscreants scattered as he approached with his "Chief Is In" sign. With reporters and photographers milling around, Thayer set up a lawn chair and sat down, waving at passing motorists and speaking to residents walking by. For now, he surmised, the drug dealers were on their heels. For now, he was commanding this symbolic slice of turf. The media loved his gumption and the message concerning right and wrong, momentarily ridding the neighborhood of the worst possible element, and being a proactive police organization.

Evans did not mind the chief's forays, either. The exposure and initiative were essentially free. In fact, as the years went on, Evans permitted Siebert to spend more of his time at the police department rather than city hall. The department was fighting to earn respect, escape from years of antagonism between the city and the newspapers, and inform the public that the Manson County Sheriff's Office was not the only viable local law enforcement agency.

Chief Ballentine had disliked "perp walks"—something offended him about the way they were orchestrated by Siebert to attract media attention. But there was little he could say to Siebert, who worked directly for the mayor. When Thayer became chief, the practice was commonplace, a publicity goldmine. Detectives Pradley and Spangler often investigated the high-octane cases most compatible with the walks; they were frequently photographed by Tallemay Bay media escorting the suspects from the police department across the parking lot to a marked patrol unit displaying the "Brannon Police" logo for transport to the county jail.

Detective Spangler, in particular, seemed to take pride in the walks. If the city and police administration did not reward his efforts with more pay, at least he could garner public recognition for putting another "scumbag" behind bars. He or Pradley would call Siebert if they had a particularly interesting or atrocious suspect in custody, giving him an estimate of how long it would take to conduct interviews (called interrogation in a less politically correct era), complete paperwork, and arrange for transport. Once the time frame was secured, Siebert contacted all area media to inform them of the general circumstances surrounding the arrest and when they could expect to obtain visuals of the suspect. A standard press release and mug shot usually accompanied the walk, followed by Siebert's statements to the media, crafted carefully according to what Spangler and Pradley said could be released without undermining the investigation.

The walks took place despite publicly convicting the suspect without a trial. The cops, however, were confident that most, if not all, the suspects were deserving of arrest and worse. Years earlier, showing the faces of juvenile suspects had been against the law, but much to the satisfaction of law enforcement personnel, legislation was passed making it legal. Indeed, many of the worst criminals in Brannon were juveniles with remarkably long criminal histories. The police were often rankled by the "soft" treatment given habitual juvenile criminals by judges.

Many of the juveniles became arrogant, knowing the system would coddle them until the age of eighteen. One sixteen-year-old was arrested for armed robbery, attempted murder and aggravated assault. The street punks called him "Demon" because he was a "bad ass" with little discernible respect for human life. His walk to the patrol car was an expletive-laced media circus, especially when the handcuffed "Demon" managed to pull down his pants and moon the photographers. Spangler and Pradley remained stoic, placing him in the cruiser without a word or change of expression. In keeping with police perceptions, "Demon" was soon returned to civilization thanks to lenient judges and statutes governing juveniles. Siebert asked the detectives what would have happened to "Demon" had he mocked or confronted Al Dillard, a somewhat notorious sheriff's deputy from the past: Dillard, they said, would have thrown the teenager down the back steps of the detective division and told everyone "Demon" simply had the misfortune of losing his balance, a fate richly deserved in the minds of most officers.

Lengthy criminal histories followed four juveniles who cursed reporters as they were escorted out of police headquarters on a sweltering afternoon in Brannon. Siebert had called the assortment of media only three hours earlier—the foursome had allegedly stolen cars, robbed businesses and burglarized residences. It dawned on him that one reporter in particular, Connie Kim of the *Tribune*, might write a story sympathetic to the plight of police officers fighting a revolving door of juvenile justice. Kim appeared to be refreshingly pro-law enforcement, something especially uncommon among newspaper reporters. Knowing it was unlawful as police spokesman to reveal the criminal histories of juveniles to the media or public, he deftly challenged her to verify their records at the courthouse. He also provided her quotes about how frustrated police can be with other branches of the criminal justice system for perpetuating juvenile lawlessness. It was a terrific article, from a police perspective, with the headline "Four youths are arrested—again." In addition, not being a sworn officer and working for the mayor enabled him to be more candid, perhaps, than police personnel who interfaced with prosecutors, public defenders, caseworkers and judges. The suspects had reason to smile, however: none of them faced serious jail time until they committed crimes as eighteen-year-old adults.

Police officers must defend themselves against difficult odds, and sometimes the urgency of the moment supersedes discipline and restraint learned in law enforcement academies. One day, Pradley was serving an arrest warrant on a wealthy slumlord for thirteen counts of attempted murder after the man tried to burn down one of his own buildings with migrant worker tenants inside. The accused arsonist had struck Pradley with a bottle and punched him several times as the detective was attempting to make the arrest. Andrew Carey also unleashed his Bull Mastiff on Pradley, who was in a terrifying fight for survival. Pradley later told Siebert that conventional tactics are not always sufficient during a violent altercation. Prompted by the wanton viciousness of the assault and a robust adrenalin rush, he not only injured but handcuffed the suspect before other officers arrived on scene. The detective sustained a fractured wrist, cuts, puncture wounds, and scars for the rest of his life.

Carey was not the only criminal accustomed to enlisting dogs such as pit bulls and Rottweilers to intimidate law enforcement. Officers shot several such animals when they were being attacked approaching drug dens or trying to corner a suspect. The Brannon Police Department purchased several Hungarian German Shepherds trained in narcotics detection, search and rescue, and enforcement. A jet-black K-9 named Bear actually outflanked a pit bull, emasculating his backside.

Detective Tom Schmidt, a Floridian with limited tolerance, yielded his badge and gun to his comrades at the police department so that he could be left alone in an interrogation room to confront an alleged crack cocaine dealer who had been threatening him with bodily harm from the moment he was arrested. The individual lost his bravado, refusing to fight the incensed officer.

"You might be laughing now, but pretty soon you'll be wearing pink panties in prison." That was the refrain of Capt. Larry Robertson, one of the few African-Americans on the Brannon police force, as sixteen-year-old Tony Taylor was preparing for his walk to the cruiser. A bevy of reporters and photographers were waiting to see the person accused of a headline-grabbing crime rampage.

Pradley's ability to elicit dialogue from alleged criminals was evident in the case of Taylor, a disturbingly violent juvenile who was eventually tried as an adult and dispatched to the state penitentiary for life. Taylor and an assortment of accomplices went on a shooting and robbing spree of several weeks. In the tradition of a shoot 'em up cowboy from an old western movie, the skinny, boyish African-American teenager from a small rural community forty-five minutes away would exit crime scenes by firing his gun into the air.

Taylor's escapades left one victim face down in his doorway after cashing his paycheck from working long hours at the citrus plant. A couple of other victims were thugs who crossed his path over money and drugs. But Pradley's break in the case came when Taylor and thirty-year-old Jermaine Blevins broke into the house of former city council member Alfred McKenzie. Blevins had worked for McKenzie at his large, impoverished eastside apartment complex, and knew when his former boss arrived home with rent money.

They were waiting for McKenzie outside the house, held him up at gunpoint, and then ushered him inside. While Taylor was ransacking the place, McKenzie mustered the courage to attack Blevins in the living room, but Blevins shot him once in the chest. Fortunately, McKenzie's daughter was able to obtain the license number from McKenzie's get-away car. McKenzie survived the shooting, probably because he was extremely overweight.

Pradley tracked the plate to Blevins and went looking for

the suspects in their tiny, moribund home town. Pradley immediately contacted the community's only police officer, who was confident Taylor could be found in a nearby park. Sure enough, after two days of surveillance, they observed Taylor hanging out with a few friends near the basketball court. He made no attempt to flee as the officers approached. Pradley calmly told him he would like to talk about some recent events in Brannon, specifically shootings and robberies.

What followed was Taylor's confession to the crimes and several days driving around Brannon with the suspect to document the particulars. One thing was clear to Pradley: Taylor was proud of what he had done. He grinned often while speaking excitedly to the detective. In fact, the state's attorney refused to prosecute one of the shootings because Taylor's exchange with Pradley supposedly motivated him to amplify and boast too much about his achievements. Interestingly, he confessed to shooting at people, but claimed that he never waited to witness the consequences.

A couple of years later, Detective Martin Jilly became convinced Blevins was connected to several other crimes in the area and questioned him at the state prison, where he was serving time for the attempted murder of the city councilman. Blevins was not obligated to tell him anything of consequence, and he did not; instead, he threatened to hunt him down when he was released from the joint. Jilly said that was fine, that he would be waiting and derive immense pleasure from putting a bullet between his eyes. Jilly, who left law enforcement to work in a family business, also baited the convict by saying that he planned to consume a mouth-watering dinner of fried chicken and watermelon on his way back to Brannon.

One of the most bizarre and media-frenzied episodes involved a teenaged female. Siebert was sound asleep in the early morning hours when he received call from Gary Carlton, the one-man Brannon bureau chief for the CBS affiliate in Tallemay Bay. He called Carlton immediately, learning that a missing female was about to be reunited with her father in the lobby of the police department.

Siebert was more loyal to Carlton than any reporter in the area. Carlton was actually a videographer, but doubled as a reporter out of necessity, usually working alone. He could be trusted to go off the record with Siebert and other sources, generally covering Brannon municipal government in a flattering light, and laboring overtime to beat the competition. The two had met nearly ten years before when they worked at the local ABC affiliate. The bearded, six-foot-five Carlton looked more like a mountain man than a member of the media. Siebert nearly always provided him first access to alluring stories and, in this instance, Carlton was returning the favor.

Thanks to a tip from one of the Brannon patrol officers whose identity he never revealed, Carlton was on the verge of smoking the other media, something that made him ecstatic. The teenager, as it turned out, had traveled from her Port Ramos home, two hours south of Tallemay Bay, to a bodybuilding competition in North Carolina. Unfortunately, Sarah Collic was not on the bus when her father, very eager to compliment his daughter for winning first place, tried to pick her up two days earlier at the Greyhound station in Tallemay Bay so he could drive her by car to Port Ramos. He and the police feared she had been abducted. The night before she was found the story received fleeting coverage on two evening newscasts in Tallemay Bay, but few people other than the police were concerned sixty miles away in Brannon.

At around 5:00 a.m., Carlton shot video of the attractive, muscular blonde hugging her father in the presence of Siebert and a couple of uniformed cops who, with the help of informants, had found her sleeping peacefully at the home of some local drug dealers. The emotional, tearful reunion made the CBS station's morning news and sparked incredible interest in the story among competing stations that had no visuals of her.

Pradley and Jilly arrived that morning to interview the youngster about what had happened. They found her surprisingly calm and unshaken. They also determined that she had not been abducted, after all. Quite the contrary, according to Collic, she had befriended an older woman on the bus and they decided to get off at the last stop before Tallemay Bay. In conversations with Tallemay Bay detectives, Pradley ascertained the older woman was a known prostitute. Further discussion with Collic revealed they spent about forty-eight hours in Tallemay Bay and Brannon partying and having sex with a variety of men.

The story, meanwhile, became stranger when she revealed one of the men sexually assaulted her. That possibility, the sordid details of her hiatus, her status as a minor, and the wholesome, vulnerable image portrayed in her reunion with the father made life awkward for Siebert as a deluge of media swarmed around the police department. Every television station from Tallemay Bay to Port Ramos converged on Brannon. They set their cameras up in front of the department and waited—waited to photograph Collic and her father as they departed the building.

Siebert conducted interviews about the sheer relief felt by police, the father, the community, and anyone else who feared for her safety. His comments were generic, alluding not to the ugly details surrounding the case, but to the fact authorities found her unharmed. Questions about foul play were answered by saying it was an ongoing investigation and she was okay. No, he said, from all indications she was not abducted. And so on.

What they wanted most was video. Without video, Carlton and the CBS outlet had an exclusive. Naturally some of the media knew from past experience that the Brannon police were famous for "perp walks" and telling the media when to expect someone to emerge from the building.

Several hours passed because the case was so bizarre and detectives held lengthy interviews with Collic. At one point, Jilly snuck her out the back door and into his unmarked unit, so they could reconstruct where she had been in Brannon. During their ride, the detective looked into his rearview mirror and saw a television truck following them. The raw-boned, diminutive kick boxer was livid, calling Siebert instantly. "Get these fuckers out of here," he demanded. Siebert contacted the news desk at the Tallemay Bay television station, and the reporters drove back to the police department.

Jilly and the girl had also returned when Siebert told the

overzealous and frustrated media to be patient, that they were likely to get video of them exiting the building pretty soon. It never happened. Worried the slightest hitch might tip off the media, it was the only occasion in their legacy of collaborating on cases that Pradley failed to inform Siebert of what he was doing. He and Jilly secretly ushered Collic out the back door and drove her to a nearby convenience store to meet her father, who had taken a similar route to escape the gaggle of reporters.

"They're not in there, are they?"

Maybe the look on Siebert's face said it all. Profound dread followed him out the front door of the police department when he learned they were gone. One reporter, whom he knew only vaguely, shouted a couple of expletives. It had been a long, stressful day of conjecture, and Siebert reciprocated. Don't worry, a couple of reporters assured him, they would have video if it meant flying helicopters to the Collic home in Port Ramos. Some of the Tallemay Bay media made good on the promise, descending on father and daughter as they pulled into their driveway. No arrests were made in the case and, despite the frenzy, media interest dissipated rapidly.

Siebert apologized to Chief Thayer for losing his temper. The chief was gracious and understood his angry reaction to the reporter. Given how hard they had worked to build strong rapport with the Tallemay Bay television stations, however, they both called the reporter's superior to apologize. The apology was accepted despite agitation in the voice of the FOX affiliate's assignment editor.

Siebert remained uneasy about the episode, realizing he

was better off not losing his cool. He decided to seek feedback on the altercation from Nick Cell, the public information officer with the Tallemay Bay Sheriff's Office. They had spoken a couple of times at the annual PIO law enforcement state conference and gotten along well. Cell told him he had hung up on one of the FOX reporters himself because the guy was rude. He even accused him of being a lousy reporter.

"The FOX station really goes after the sensational stuff," Cell said. "They can be obnoxious because they are trying to catch up in the ratings. Don't worry about pissing them off."

Still, Siebert and Thayer made a unique public relations swing through Tallemay Bay a few months later to fortify their rapport with various stations there. Assignment editors and reporters were delighted with the plaques Thayer had presented thanking them for their excellent coverage through the years. A couple of the stations, including FOX, even ran video of the chief commending reporters and editors on the early evening news.

Siebert and Thayer understood the importance of maintaining civility with the media. On one hand, it is critical for the police to appear competent by closing cases and safeguarding the community; on the other, crime must be prevalent enough in the public mind to justify funding for personnel and resources. Part of Siebert's job was to attract media attention by peddling novel, mesmerizing crime stories that fortified the department's legacy.

An example involved Gary Hokum, a small-time crook who got hooked on crack cocaine and went on a robbery spree. Most interesting, in Siebert's mind, was his method of operation: Hokum approached bank tellers and store clerks in a jovial manner, actually smiling when he told them it was a stickup and produced a handgun. He would say something on the order of, "You won't believe it, but this is a robbery." When the number of robberies approached a dozen, Siebert decided to dub the robber the "Smiling Bandit" in an effort to entice media coverage that could assist in his capture.

It worked: following his written press release about the "Smiling Bandit" to all Tallemay Bay media, many of them converged on the police department to learn more. They wanted quotes from Siebert about the robber and rehashed the particulars of the robberies. His ability to elude capture after committing so many robberies only added to the suspense.

Siebert explained the robber was both clever and lucky, that apprehending him had been difficult because he struck a wide range of businesses at various times of day. As it happened, tips from the public were not directly responsible for Hokum's demise. A convenience store clerk, though, ostensibly decided to arm himself because of the articles and shot the "Smiling Bandit" in self-defense. Hokum's luck had run out, but the Brannon Police Department gained more desirable exposure.

"Get out of the fuckin' car! Now! Get out of the car!" Jimmy Spangler's service revolver was pointed through the window of a vehicle driven by a "John" alleged to have propositioned a female police officer masquerading as a prostitute. Prostitution stings usually followed citizens' complaints to the mayor, city council and police department about women plying the world's oldest trade on U.S. 61, a main Brannon thoroughfare lined with seedy motels, an occasional strip club, dumpy bars and liquor stores.

They also made good copy for press releases and press briefings, resulting in numerous arrests. The "clean up" purportedly demonstrated responsive government and law enforcement. For those who suggested prostitution could not possibly be controlled and that cracking down was a waste of taxpayers' money, Siebert and the chief retorted that prostitutes carry AIDS and are usually linked to other crimes such as drug trafficking and armed robbery.

Media were sometimes invited to join the cops in their "sweep" of the area, although the actual taped negotiation between the "John" and prostitute was off limits. For legal reasons, photographing the suspects was only allowed as they were being transported. Nonetheless, plenty of careers and marriages were destroyed by the public humiliation.

The actual prostitutes were occasionally busted when male police officers posed as johns. But usually they were streetwise enough to scatter like cockroaches when police descended on the area. They sometimes acted as informants, providing information about violent crimes and narcotics transactions, but their drug addictions, criminal histories and associations with pimps made them dubious allies of law enforcement.

Another disenfranchised, news making population were the homeless, who received more compassion from media and government. In concert with a federally funded initiative on homelessness, Evans began the Brannon homeless coalition comprised of local organizations and officials. Evans compelled Siebert to launch a media blitz that received outstanding coverage of the coalition's soup kitchen and shelter. The idea, of course, was to bolster the significance of the problem to potential donors.

It also raised media and public awareness about homeless people being veterans, mentally ill, recently unemployed, and crime victims rather than lazy, worthless bumpkins. The most visible homeless group, however, fit the label of middle-aged white men who drank too much, wandered the streets, and sometimes encountered common criminals. Tragically, in a case investigated by Pradley, one of the men was beaten to death in the night by a violent, recidivistic felon who learned the man had received a $50 in cash from his mother for Christmas. Another was killed by a mob of teenaged gang members, and a third hanged himself in front of the planetarium downtown.

The seamy side of homeless life was shared one day by Siebert with Carlton, the supportive Tallemay Bay television videographer-reporter. Detectives had told Siebert the story of a local deliveryman who frequently traded a cup of coffee with one of the homeless men in exchange for sniffing his anus on lunch breaks, earning the moniker "the sniffer."

The media are frequently branded for being unethical and uncaring, asking crime victims and other bereaved people "How do you feel?" in the aftermath of tragedies, but stereotypes are sometimes deceiving.

Terrance Salley had been a terrific local high school athlete who played football at Florida State University, securing a tryout with the Green Bay Packers. The media knew him as the director of the Brannon youth center on the day he learned his cousin, Vanessa Garrison, had been knifed to death by an intruder in her apartment. Siebert was already at the crime scene when Salley exited his car and rushed over to him in tears. Due to his emotion, and conceivably his status, none of the reporters at the scene asked him questions. At Siebert's behest, they backed off as Salley retreated to the office of the apartment complex to commiserate with relatives.

The teen-aged killer had casually befriended his older victim but the crime was considered random and inexplicable. Earlier the same morning, he had attacked a jogger in the same neighborhood for no apparent reason. The story made headlines, but the media's deference to Salley's privacy was nearly unprecedented. The assailant, meanwhile, was sent to prison.

Some stories were better off eluding the media. They may have wondered why the mayor tolerated frequent visits from a man in his twenties named Ron North, the nephew of city planning chief Terry North. While the mayor regarded his department head as marginally competent, at least he was generally pleasant and submissive. North's nephew, uneducated and delusional, aspired to be a prominent political figure, supposedly admiring the mayor. So, for nearly a year, he would visit the mayor on a regular basis to talk about politics and "important" city matters. The visits, though, eventually became annoying and burdensome for Evans.

Ron North was visibly angry on several occasions when Siebert and the mayor's secretary, Jenny Bowles, told him the mayor was too busy for visitors or they did not know when he would be back in the office. It likely inspired him to leave a note under the secretary's door stating she would "regret" obstructing his relationship with the mayor. Soon a security lock appeared on the door leading to the offices of the mayor, Bowles and Siebert. Believing North was deranged and potentially violent, Siebert began carrying a handgun in his briefcase. North had claimed he was meeting with the president in addition to the mayor, and that inner voices were imploring him to "fix" the political system.

Within days, Hillyard and a boyish detective with a southern twang named Kedrick Danson appeared at the door of North's Brannon apartment. The apartment managers had told the detectives North wandered around the complex at odd hours and jogged in his bikini underwear, but never thought about calling the police. Apparently, no one told them that North was a sturdy, intimidating looking individual.

He answered the door with his head shaved and did not invite them in. Hillyard and Danson showed their police identification and Hillyard told North, "We can do this the easy way or the hard way. The easy way means we are taking you down to the mental ward under the Baker Act for psychological evaluation. The hard way means we take you to jail. You can't make threats against the mayor's office."

He stared at them for what seemed like a minute, but probably was a few seconds. He backed up slowly, and let them in. As the simmering North started gathering his things, Hillyard discovered photographs on the kitchen table of the mayor, Bowles and Siebert. He obviously was obsessed with them and could have been planning to retaliate.

No charges were filed against North. Instead, he was released after spending several weeks in the mental ward. The day he was released, North called Siebert to apologize for his behavior.

"I'm leaving town. I just want to make sure you guys won't put me in jail. I never want to go to jail."

"Nothing bad will happen, Ron, as long as you just get on with your life. Good things can happen to you."

"Thanks. I won't be back."

He kept his promise, although Siebert looked over his shoulder for the next several months. Terry North later told Evans and Siebert his nephew was living on the streets of Tallemay Bay and practically lost his ear in an attack by an alligator near a retention pond, a sad but highly entertaining story at city hall.

The media never learned of the Bonnie Konslaw saga, either, because it was handled internally. Konslaw worked as a "meter lady" for the police department's parking division while seeking certification to be a police officer. She reported checking a meter downtown when a man across the street supposedly began yelling things like, "I love your hair," "I know who you are," "Don't' worry, nobody will catch me," and "I'll be watching you." Her description of the man was vague and the cops were unable to locate him.

She also called the department complaining of harassing notes left on her car and the porch of her home. The notes examined by Pradley appeared to be cut-and-paste from periodicals such as magazines and newspapers: "We are going to really hurt you," "I want to crème in you," "Watch for any unexpected changes," "You make me mad," "Hidden gifts," and "Did you like my big dick?" A note taped to a parking meter read, "We are really going to hurt you, girl."

The notes were submitted by Pradley for fingerprint processing but revealed nothing. After a Barbie Doll was found on her doormat with its legs spread, police began surveillance of her home. In addition, she claimed someone was calling her home to say, "We are going to get you." Another note on her police motor scooter read, "Nobody will catch me" and included excerpts of a poem about death.

Things allegedly worsened when she reported being attacked in the city parking garage. She said someone wearing black leather gloves pushed her against the wall from behind, sticking a hard object against her tailbone. The assailant ran away, according to her story, and she radioed police. Four units arrived quickly but no suspect was apprehended.

During his conversations with the woman, Pradley learned she had never been raped but said maybe if she were, the harassment would go away. She also confessed to having an affair with fellow recruit Matt Kirley at the police academy. She said he had broken up with her, and that he was the most likely culprit in the threats and assault. But Pradley became more suspicious of her when officers setting up a phone tap at her home discovered cut-and-pasted materials similar to those used in the notes. She did not receive any more calls, either.

Kirley passed a polygraph test, and she became irate when asked by Pradley to take one. Then the hysterical woman admitted to writing some, but not all, of the notes, and promised never to lie again. If that were not enough, Konslaw began denying she had an affair and making claims they had never broken up. Due to her inconsistent remarks and conduct, and Pradley's report to the chief, she was terminated by the department and soon dropped out of the police academy.

Another case that remained in-house began in the early morning hours on the city's forlorn east side. A drug dealer was being chased on foot by four uniformed officers and their commander, Sgt. Will Tovar. When the suspect tripped over a fence and fell to the ground, he was struck repeatedly with a flashlight, suffering deep lacerations to his head.

According to Pradley, who was freighted with investigating what actually transpired in the booking room, the sergeant convinced the man to sign a statement that his injuries resulted from the fall, not a beating. The mayor and police administrators had expected quick resolution, but Pradley arrested the offending officer, Peter Jacobs, for criminal battery, implicating the others for falsifying evidence, criminal misconduct, and violating civil rights.

Unable or unwilling to craft a just, tangible resolution, and fearing the wrath of city hall, two high-ranking police officials resigned for "health and personal" reasons. Most of the officers in question, including the sergeant, were quietly returned to regular duty. Jacobs was terminated. Several months later, the city bequeathed the victim and his outraged family a sizeable sum of money, essentially making the case go away.

CHAPTER FOUR

SABOTAGING THE SEX CRIMES STORY

"**YOU'LL NEVER GUESS** who we've got in custody."

"Who?"

"He's the photography editor at the newspaper."

"For what?"

"Sex crimes. Sex with minors."

While Siebert's brief phone conversation that evening with Pradley was intriguing, it was impossible to fathom the magnitude of a story that could have been fodder for national tabloids. Major newspapers and magazines wrote about the "Telly" Schmitz case. Most of the coverage, however, was confined to Tallemay Bay, one of the largest media markets in the nation. The case would have political repercussions in the community for at least a decade, placing the police in the middle of a traditionally caustic relationship between Brannon municipal government and the *Herald*.

Other local and regional media were apparently unaware of the arrest until the *Herald* published a brief story the next morning. The lead generically mentioned his arrest. Two paragraphs later readers learned the individual was actually graphics editor of the newspaper. The public information officer was quoted as saying that the initial charges of one count of sexual performance with a child, one count of producing or directing sexual performance with a child, one count of possession of a video in reference to sexual performance of a child and four counts of sexual activity with a child against Schmitz involved two girls between the ages of twelve and seventeen.

Pradley had studied psychology prior to becoming a cop, earning a reputation for being thorough and professional, possessing a low-key demeanor and ability to coax confessions out of suspects, skills that would be crucial from the outset of the Schmitz case.

Pradley told Siebert police received their first lead when a woman showed up at the police department with a video of a fourteen-year-old girl simulating oral sex and displaying her breasts. Police called Schmitz at his office to express concerns about the tape. Pradley and Hillyard initially interviewed the drawn, balding Schmitz at the police department, where he indicated he had done things he was not proud of but had difficulty discussing them. When confronted with the videotape, he confessed to shooting the video. He denied having sexual contact with the juvenile females, but said there were photographs he was willing to relinquish at his office and home.

Pradley and Hillyard followed Schmitz up the backstairs

of the *Herald* building and proceeded to the photo lab adjacent to the newsroom. The subdued Schmitz began rifling through his desk, producing envelopes labeled "modeling" which contained portfolio style photographs of the girls in varying degrees of undress. It would turn out to be one of several visits to the newspaper.

Schmitz's house was difficult to see from the road. It was near an inlet, surrounded by thick foliage and palm trees. The interior was cramped and cluttered with furniture placed randomly and magazines stacked everywhere. A narrow staircase made its way up the two-and-a-half story structure. Schmitz lived in the house with his wife and two stepdaughters, none of whom were home. Dressed in shorts and t-shirt, the disheveled suspect with a ponytail looked much older than his forty-three years but seemed fairly calm for someone who must have known he was in serious trouble.

Pradley figured Schmitz might relax even more if they sat down to talk casually at a picnic table in the back yard. Hillyard remained inside the house. Pradley banked on a non-confrontational strategy with the suspect. They had no search warrant; a mood change could make Schmitz stop cooperating and ask them to leave. He could not appear judgmental about the suspect. Pradley needed to break the ice. They talked about his job. Schmitz was proud of his innovative photographic abilities. Rubbing his goatee, he explained that black and white film is actually more artistic than color in the creative process, and therefore less pornographic. They discussed children and raising teenagers. He clearly enjoyed talking about himself. He admitted there were things he kept to himself and, slowly but surely, started opening up about the sex crimes.

"You have been lucky to enjoy the freedom of your lifestyle," Pradley mused. "Most of us really hate what we're doing; most of us don't enjoy our lives very much. You are evidently very smart and artistic."

Schmitz managed a smile. There was something almost juvenile about the man. Pradley surmised he and many other pedophiles had not matured sexually beyond the age of their victims. Pradley realized Schmitz and his wife, Terry, lived in a fantasy world, dressing up as magicians at the Sand Key medieval fair. She wrote a column on astrology for the *Herald.* He had an "all seeing eye" drawn in the middle of his right palm.

"Hey, I like watching (young) girls walk topless around the house," Schmitz explained. "They were usually willing to 'lend a hand,' if you will." The connotation of his remark made him smile again.

Pradley smiled also. Schmitz kept talking. He mentioned the peepholes in his home that enabled him to observe the girls in the nude or modest attire and violate their privacy. "They would have been pretty upset had they known about them," he said with a laugh. Pradley laughed, too.

He said he had lied about not having sexual contact with the girls. He confessed to having sex with one of the victims more than two hundred times. In addition, he admitted to having sexual intercourse during the past few years with other minors, two of whom he victimized at the same party in a hot tub at his residence. Pradley listened patiently as the revelations surfaced. It was important for the detective not to show the utter revulsion and anger he felt toward Schmitz. The guy was obviously a real creep, someone deserving of life behind bars. Or worse.

Schmitz went on to say that many of the photographs had been shot at the newspaper. Schmitz exuded a sense of relief, telling Pradley it was comforting talking to someone and that he thought his day was getting better. He appeared remorseful and, as they stood up from the picnic table, gave Pradley a hug.

His remorse seemed to fade when they went back inside the house and he proudly showed Pradley the peepholes. It reminded Pradley of a classmate in junior high school who watched his sisters through peepholes as a prank. Schmitz was almost giddy talking about them. It made him feel clever. It was almost as though he viewed his conduct as fun rather than criminal.

"I believe what you are saying but I will have to convince my bosses it was all harmless fun," Pradley explained. "The woman who showed us the tape from the party gave us some statements that might suggest otherwise."

"I am an artist. You will understand me if you view the photographs that way. They are art work."

Hillyard told them he had found several rolls of film and torn photographs in a wastebasket. Schmitz reasoned that he had thrown out the film because he knew the police would not like it. Repeating that he was an artist, Schmitz said there was more film the officers might want to retrieve at the newspaper.

It was clear to Pradley that Schmitz had an inner drive to make people see things his way. He felt sorry for himself and wanted to explain that he was not a bad person. He kept telling Pradley how to convey his predicament to the authorities, and trusted the detective's contention that more information was needed to do so. They had developed a bond that Schmitz would regret.

Again, with Schmitz's cooperation and no search warrant, they drove the suspect to the *Herald* building, where he turned over thousands of incriminating photographs and negatives, many of which were supposedly taken of stoned and intoxicated under-aged females on the premises. Most of them were stored in his employee locker. The officers helped Schmitz carry several boxes of photographs and negatives to their unmarked police unit.

Pradley and Hillyard continued their interview with Schmitz at the police department, where the appalling details continued to unfold. Among the items recovered by police was a diary of his sexual activities with the victims, using at least fifteen different symbols to portray various sexual acts and conduct. Some symbols reflected whether the victims were in the mood to have sexual relations with Schmitz or menstruating.

A short time later, two of Schmitz's victims nervously came to the police department, verifying what he had told the detectives. The photographs helped the girls identify other victims, most of whom were later contacted and interviewed by police. Detectives filed many of the more damning charges against Schmitz according to the nature of the sexual contact described by the victims. While Schmitz thought he had kept his cherished peepholes a secret, the victims actually confirmed their existence to Pradley.

Siebert recalled what Pradley had told him in the past: investigators must be good actors. As their trust and working relationship evolved, Pradley became more forthcoming to Siebert about his techniques. Pradley said he would never condone the crime, but give it some rationalization to minimize the consequences in the suspect's mind. He would tell suspects he was there to help, assist in the court system and perhaps offer a solution. In one instance, he told a suspect that shooting a 7-Eleven clerk in the arm was better than shooting him in the head; shooting him in the head would have meant more trouble with the law. And, had the clerk cooperated, perhaps the shooting would not have been necessary. After all, so the logic frequently goes with suspects, everyone makes mistakes.

"It is hard not to tell someone like Schmitz that he is a piece of shit," Pradley conceded. "When I get close to telling someone that, I try to concentrate on the victims and how badly they need me to get information from the bad guy."

It was probably ironic that the police department, rather than the larger, more media friendly Manson County sheriff's office three blocks away, had jurisdiction over the case. The city had been bludgeoned by the newspaper for years, largely because of the disdain its editors felt for Mayor Evans. Among other things, editorials had referred to him as a dictator, Mussolini, the Ayatollah. and a bully. Indeed, slashed tires and a broken window on his car failed to dissuade him from deflating union proponents at the police department years earlier. He hired the city's first designated public information officer because of a mortifying water contamination crisis and the relationship they had established when Siebert was a local television reporter covering council meetings.

Needless to say, the mayor's negative feelings about the *Herald* and the *Tribune* sometimes made the PIO's job especially difficult. On some days, Evans laughed off derogatory articles: "To Hell with them. It doesn't matter what they say about us." On other occasions, however, every inch of his massive body would flush with red: "Can you believe what those bastards are saying? They weren't elected to run the goddamn city. I was." His sentiments, in combination with Siebert's desire to maintain some civility with the newspaper reporters, could be a conundrum. One reporter told Siebert that his superiors, including executive editor Warren Posley, warned him about the city and its evil mayor when he assumed the beat. In a certain regard, Siebert admired the mayor's courage to repel ongoing newspaper assaults on the city when other government entities seemingly got a pass. The mayor believed he could offset the negative newspaper coverage by cultivating positive rapport with area television stations, something Siebert thought they were pretty successful doing. The mayor figured the "newspaper folks" could watch positive stories about the city on the six o'clock news.

Despite perceptions to the contrary, the mayor stayed away from the Schmitz case. Most public statements came from the PIO. They never strategized media relations regarding Schmitz. As police spokesman, Siebert was working initially with Ballentine who, while generally avoiding the media, was forced momentarily into the spotlight because of allegations the paper lodged against the police department. Ballentine also got to know the PIO when he was a television reporter, but probably would have been happier had Siebert not introduced a more aggressive approach to malign the newspaper's behavior surrounding Schmitz.

Schmitz was not formally charged until that evening, allowing him a relatively inconspicuous walk to the police vehicle and transport to the county jail. His mugshot and story, though, would soon resonate on prime-time television and radio newscasts and dominate newspaper headlines in Tallemay Bay.

The story simmered until two days later, when an article in the *Herald* quoted its publisher, Dolly Rittner, as saying the police may have conducted an illegal search of Schmitz's work area. She referred to the First Amendment and the sanctity of the newspaper. She was upset that Schmitz led detectives through the back door of the newspaper building. In the article, Chief Ballentine accused Rittner of trying to "kill the messenger" and countered that Schmitz volunteered to relinquish the files. In addition, on the basis of information detectives provided, Siebert, emboldened to seize the reins concerning the media, was quoted in the article as saying there were new leads and allegations in the case.

Siebert's initial reaction to the article was outrage, driven in part by a very real dislike for the newspaper's treatment of the city and the police department in the past. It was getting personal. He believed the publisher was deflecting attention from the serious charges plaguing Schmitz, a raging pedophile, to alleged chicanery and incompetence of the police officers. She was also undoubtedly attempting to protect her turf and employees against the police. Siebert wanted to defend the detectives who were mostly, in his mind, forthright and diligent.

Pradley and Hillyard were certainly working hard. Their ambition as police officers was to build their case against the suspect and track enough information to locate other potential victims regardless of the media and political fallout. A school resource officer told Pradley he had been suspicious of Schmitz because he would pick up different girls from the schools at all hours of the day. Some would even give him a kiss. The officer had also observed one of the girls bringing "modeling" photos to the school. In addition, a crime victim's advocate informed Pradley that a source told her adults had attended "borderline" parties at the Schmitz home where child pornography was displayed.

They interviewed several *Herald* employees including Randi Siegenthaler, a graphic artist who worked closely with Schmitz. She said they were good friends, and that she would often smoke marijuana with Schmitz and supply him with prescription medicines. She recalled seeing him on numerous occasions in the photo studio with young girls. She denied, however, seeing any nude photographs. Another member of Schmitz's staff, photographer Gilbert Roby, admitted that he and the suspect had been friends while growing up together in Michigan. In fact, Schmitz contacted him and about the job at the newspaper, encouraging him to move south. Roby said he was aware that Schmitz took nude photographs of adults, not children. He added that it was "common knowledge" at the newspaper that Schmitz conducted private photo sessions in the photo lab. Under questioning, he was able to identify a juvenile from one of the photos but said he was unaware of any state statutes governing child pornography.

Former *Herald* employee Madeline Tesar also said the photographic "sessions" with nude females and Schmitz were frequently joked about in the office. She said she was terminated shortly after complaining to the personnel director of the newspaper about Schmitz sexually harassing her and asking if she would smoke pot with him. She reported telling Rittner during her exit interview about "emotional problems" Schmitz apparently had with females. Another woman, Barbara Silverman of the photo department, told Pradley her repeated complaints to newspaper management that she was being sexually harassed by Schmitz and Roby were to no avail. She claimed her superiors forced her to leave the newspaper because of her allegations.

Pradley informed Siebert that dozens of additional charges were being contemplated against Schmitz. He had also been accused of sodomizing a boy on vacation several years earlier in a local park but the alleged victim's parents refused to press charges and returned home. A couple of reporters told detectives they never said anything to upper management but thought it strange that Schmitz would show up at the office in the evening with young girls. One said Schmitz would lead young girls into the photo lab between the hours of 6:30 and 9:30 on weeknights, lock the door and play music at a high volume. Other allegations surfaced, including one that executive editor Warren Posley, regarded by the mayor as an incendiary antagonist but purportedly a cordial old acquaintance of Sheriff Chas

Wellman, sometimes smoked marijuana on the loading dock of the newspaper.

The Schmitz arrest was on the cusp of becoming a mega story and the largest child molestation case in the history of the community. The new charges would be official Friday morning, at which time Siebert decided to hold a press conference. He thought intensely about the press conference that night at home. Should he mention the former employees? After all, they were not making allegations regarding Schmitz and minors. They might also have an agenda against the paper. At the same time, he believed they were germane to the story, i.e. someone had allegedly raised concerns about Schmitz in the past. He understood the media would scrutinize his every word. In addition, the *Herald* was a corporate newspaper whose attorneys would be listening. He also felt the new charges might underscore the legitimacy of the investigation and embarrass the publisher for turning against the police department. And yes, he derived some pleasure in knowing the very newspaper that delighted in myriad stories denigrating city government would now be under the duress of the police investigation and media scrutiny.

The press conference at city hall was covered by most of the regional Tallemay Bay media, not to mention the local papers and television station. Siebert had contacted the media in advance, realizing few news organizations could ignore such an unusual and titillating story. The mayor was out of town "on business." The chief preferred to stay at the police department. The detectives furnished Siebert with information that morning but did not attend. Siebert believed the sensitive nature of the case required one voice. He was on his own, facing a bevy cameras and questions. In addition to dispatching a reporter to take notes, the *Herald* recorded the entire press conference. Incredibly, there were seventy-five additional charges levied against Schmitz, including several counts of capital sexual battery with a child under the age of twelve. According to the *Herald* reporter, Betty Muir, Siebert's statement that upper management had been apprised of concerns about Schmitz in the past launched the publisher, Posley and managing editor Doug Bell into a meeting behind closed doors following the press conference. Siebert carefully phrased his remarks so that no mention of "minors" and prior complaints could be attributed to him. It would have been inaccurate, a sure-fire opening for corporate legal counsel. Indeed, the two former female employees were adults voicing concerns about Schmitz's conduct toward them. The actual charges, meanwhile, pertained to sex crimes against minors. It was a critical distinction. Siebert also mentioned that many of the crimes were actually committed in the photo lab at the paper, further inflaming the crisis.

Once again, the case was becoming toxic. Siebert probably would never have mentioned upper management at the newspaper had the publisher not berated Brannon police officers in the article two days earlier. The mutual hostility was mounting faster than the charges against Schmitz. A couple of co-workers half-jokingly told Siebert the editors would probably direct reporters to start following him around. To his knowledge, it never happened. He did, however, momentarily stop having lunch with a sports writer from the *Herald*. The Schmitz case was onerous for all concerned.

With the charges mounting, the *Herald* fired Schmitz that afternoon. Siebert could only imagine the besieged *Herald* brass when several Tallemay Bay television stations went live that night from the front lawn of the newspaper. The story was mushrooming before their eyes. Their reputation was on the line.

The *Herald's* coverage the next morning announced the additional charges and quoted the publisher as saying none of the upper management knew of any suspicions regarding Schmitz. She said items were moved out of Schmitz's work bay so that no one could tamper with them. Contrary to Siebert's allegations, Rittner maintained the newspaper was cooperating fully with the police.

"Buddy, you've got brass balls."

Those words by Sheriff Chas Wellman were music to Siebert's ears. The sheriff he revered, whom he had known as a reporter and worked for briefly in public information, had called to pay him a compliment. This was the man who lobbied tirelessly to make sure recidivistic violent criminals served at least eighty-five percent of their sentences. It was obvious that Wellman, who referred to the media sardonically as the Fourth Estate, was pleased that Siebert had challenged the *Herald* with allegations about its editors even though they generally left his agency alone. The truth was, Wellman had developed a strong rapport with the local newspapers, but did not especially like them.

"I couldn't get away with criticizing them that way," he said.

"Well, you know the mayor, and he doesn't care. Sheriff, these guys (the newspaper) asked for it. They are placing all of the blame on us."

From the beginning, the publisher had been the exclusive spokesperson for the newspaper. And, from the beginning, she vilified the police while publicly expressing no obvious compassion for Schmitz's alleged victims. The pattern continued the following day in a lengthy column by Rittner comparing Sgt. Friday of *Dragnet* fame to the wayward Brannon police. She said the police probably resented past coverage of rogue cops and missing evidence (narcotics) from the department's property room.

There is an old adage that you can't argue with someone who purchases ink "by the barrel," something the mayor would learn the hard way several years later. During the Schmitz case, however, an array of media covered all sides of the story. And, to the credit of the *Herald,* it published a letter from Chief Ballentine defending his department to the hilt. Once again, he accused the paper of trying to deflect the charges against Schmitz to the conduct of the police. In a letter published next to the chief's, however, the relative of one *Herald* employee compared the Brannon police to the Gestapo.

"I don't want any guns or badges showing."

The chief's sentiments reflected a desire to diffuse hard feelings with *Herald* editors and reporters as officers prepared to serve a search warrant at the newspaper. Some of the officers were clearly irritated by the chief's directive, which appeared to grant the paper preferential treatment over other people and organizations. The mayor was particularly angry when he learned the next day what the chief had said. In addition, Ballentine called the publisher in advance to let her know the officers were leaving for the *Herald* in a few minutes. He was on the home stretch of his tenure at the Brannon Police Department. Belying his letter to the editor and gruff law enforcement voice, Ballentine appeared eager to avoid confrontation and accommodate the newspaper's wishes due to its position in the community.

Pradley, Hillyard, three other Brannon police officers in jackets and ties and one uniformed officer went to the newspaper, where an employee at the entrance told them to wait for Rittner in a conference room. Pradley felt they were losing control of the situation, risking their ability to carry out the warrant unencumbered. He momentarily walked back outside in disgust. Vying to maintain control of her domain, the blonde, middle-aged publisher was clearly agitated and very assertive when she appeared several minutes later. She informed the officers that Schmitz's materials had been boxed up and newspaper employees would escort them to his work bay. Officers also rechecked his locker, in addition to the photo lab and studio.

Roby, Schmitz's old friend, shot numerous photographs of the officers while they were on the premises. He was especially prolific photographing a state police technician attempting to disconnect and seize Schmitz's computer as possible evidence germane to the investigation. The scene was also tense because several *Herald* employees were hooting at the police. But it grew uglier when detective Hillyard threatened to arrest Rittner for obstruction if she did not stop talking incessantly to the officers and standing in their way at the computer. She loudly protested the search and quoted the First Amendment.

Moments later, a corporate attorney representing the newspaper informed Hillyard by phone that the judge who had signed the search warrant was now limiting the scope of the computer search because it contained materials needed to publish upcoming editions of the newspaper. Ultimately the wishes of the judge in concert with corporate legal counsel precluded the police from removing and further examining the computer.

Pradley told Rittner it was unfortunate that foregoing the computer search and seizure could exempt investigators from identifying other victims; that very often pedophiles stored incriminating evidence and information on computers. She continued her harangue about the First Amendment and computer files that were imperative to printing upcoming editions of the newspaper.

A couple of days later, Pradley and Hillyard returned to the *Herald* in hopes of convincing Rittner to provide a written statement about who was involved in collecting Schmitz's work materials and disabling his computer. Rittner agreed, and employees told the investigators they abided her instructions about four hours before the search warrant was served. In addition, Rittner turned over a military style coat Schmitz often wore in the photo lab. The coat had not been considered evidence at first, but photos indicated it was often the only article of clothing worn by Schmitz's victims during "sessions" at the newspaper.

The Schmitz case splattered across a Sunday section of the *Tallemay Bay Times*, one of the most decorated and aggressive newspapers in the country. Brannon and Manson County were on the outside fringes of its circulation area. Siebert had been leery when the *Times* reporter descended on his office for an interview. He made sure chief detective Wally Wallace was there to field any allegations or questions about the searches, illegal or otherwise. He continued to say that the first visit to the newspaper was not a search. Rather, he said, Schmitz voluntarily showed detectives his work bay. The reporter also wondered what the city thought about corporate attorneys who fired off a letter demanding documentation of assertions regarding two former female employees. Siebert replied that the investigation was ongoing, meaning that certain information could not be revealed.

Siebert apprehensively opened the *Times* the day the story was published. Anyone who has been interviewed by the media can surely relate to such fear. He probably suspected the *Times* might slant its coverage against the police because the credibility of another newspaper was at stake. Wallace had predicted there would likely be "honor among thieves." The *Sabella Tribune*, for instance, had been strangely silent about the Schmitz case, probably not wanting to offend its "competitive" cohorts in the local market. Fortunately, the *Times* coverage was very balanced. It focused on the irony of a media organization becoming the story. For the first time publicly, Rittner conveyed remorse for the alleged victims. She and Siebert traded barbs, alluding to past disagreements between the city and the newspaper. In the article, Siebert wondered how Schmitz's behavior at the paper could have gone undetected. Rittner was annoyed that the police showed up at the newspaper only five minutes after the chief called to warn her in advance of the final search. The detectives, of course, felt the paper was fortunate to receive a warning. In theory, they could have entered the building, read the warrant to the wall, and proceeded with the search.

A prominent *Washington Post* columnist interviewed Siebert about the Schmitz case by phone. Like the *Times* reporter, he provided objective coverage, juggling the publisher's and Siebert's perspectives. The gist of his article was that the Schmitz case hit awfully close to home for media organizations. Once again, the fact that a newspaper had become so much of the story probably deflected from the staggering volume of charges against Schmitz. A significant piece also appeared in a national photography magazine, mostly mirroring basics of the case with supposition about ethical concerns.

Schmitz entered a guilty plea and was sentenced to life. The paper was sued by a couple of his victims. Rittner took a job in the non-profit sector as a fundraiser only months after the story simmered down. Her departure was portrayed by the *Herald* as a voluntary, irresistible opportunity for career advancement. In reality, a couple of newspaper insiders and Sheriff Wellman told Siebert the corporation forced her out the door because she mishandled public relations in the Schmitz case. Perhaps Siebert could have been less inflammatory in some of his remarks about the paper. In turn, Rittner was foolish to concentrate more heavily on the conduct of the police than the fact Schmitz purportedly committed some of the crimes at the newspaper and victimized under-aged females. Few people are tolerant of pedophiles. To some extent, in Siebert's mind, the newspaper's editors were defiant because most media are unaccustomed to being flogged in public. Needless to say, the contentious relationship that had festered over the years profoundly impacted the interaction of media and government during this tragic case. It also aggravated hard feelings between the city, the police and the newspaper in the future, solidifying its mission to topple Mayor Evans.

CHAPTER FIVE

PUBLIC JOURNALISM AND THE PUBLIC SAFETY COMPLEX

THE *BRANNON HERALD* called Mayor Evans all sorts of things, most of them derogatory, but detractors and apologists alike knew him as Boss Hog or Bulldozer Will. Through political fortitude, efficiency, intimidation and reducing taxes each year of his administration, Evans had transformed a theoretically strong council form of government into a prevailing mayor regime in practice. The ex-cop had run unsuccessfully for county commission and the school board prior to becoming mayor, a position he flourished and reveled in. He was elected by landslide margins every four years but always ran aggressively by going door to door, especially on the pledge of not raising taxes in the more conservative retirement communities that were a bastion of unwavering support.

His name, in many regards, was synonymous with Brannon. When some Manson County officials were advocating government consolidation, Evans leaned on them with every ounce of his ample girth to preserve the city. And when the county commission hesitated to approve a permit for construction of the Wilson Evans Reservoir, the mayor threatened to personally start bulldozing the site with the help of his public works director. He also began a crusade challenging proposed rate hikes by state water districts. The *Herald* wrote a scathing editorial about Siebert's press releases promoting Evans's vow to debate anyone connected with the water districts because they referred to him frequently as the "Honorable Mayor" Evans. The editorial did not believe the mayor was deserving of the salutation and wondered if an Evans "cult" was in the making. It also accused Siebert of angling for an Oscar with the hyperbole in the releases. It referred to Siebert as the mayor's "flack" producing "self-puffing" press releases. But the controversial mayor from Brannon was a formidable adversary, even becoming president of the state's League of Cities organization.

One thing was certain: Mayor Evans never ran away from a good scrap. Al Church, a city councilman and full-time school teacher, found himself pinned against the wall after a city council meeting because he accused Evans of fomenting corruption at the police department. He liked to tell city hall insiders how pleasurable it would be to "whip the asses" of every editor at the *Herald* who criticized him. While a state trooper, Evans actually called out an editor at the

Sabella Journal who allegedly misrepresented facts about a criminal investigation.

The mayor could be bombastic and intimidating, but had no airs. He was often ungrammatical, rarely wore ties and dressed like an average Joe. He drove to work in a faded blue old Cadillac with papers and litter in the back seat. Each morning at 9:00, he parked in his assigned space at city hall and lumbered to the elevator for the ride to his second-floor office.

His political instincts rarely backfired; those he treated fairly normally remained loyal. One notable exception, in Evans's mind, was city councilman Gino Garagolo. The mayor had engineered his promotion to fire chief many years earlier and encouraged him to run for office under the assumption he would generally endorse his policies and administration. Instead, Garagolo became an alleged turncoat, plotting to run for mayor and cavorting with *Herald* editor Warren Posley, a man plainly determined to destroy Evans's regime. Garagolo had been seen in Posley's office on several occasions, according to reporters who knew Siebert. In addition, as suspicions evolved, Siebert listened to him speaking amicably to the reviled editor over the phone. Jenny Bowles, the mayor's administrative assistant, would shake her head and ask incredulously, "Can you believe that Gino Garagolo? Isn't he horrible? How can he behave this way after all the mayor has done for him?"

Garagolo, a snarky cop hater, decided against running for mayor after testing the political waters. He and Evans had plenty of mutual friends, the majority of whom would ultimately stand by the mayor. One day the mayor spouted his familiar retort to Garagolo: "Go ahead and run, Gino, because I'm going enjoy kicking your ass." Regardless, Garagolo continued to rebuff the mayor covertly.

The saga of the public safety complex began at the mayor's behest. For years he had run the city on a tight budget, savaging the colossal salaries and fancy digs of other local governments. He howled at the "waste" committed by the school system, county government, and even his former police chief, Sheriff Chas Wellman. In fact, he and Walz frivolously threw play money in the air at a county commission meeting. The city accumulated a startling reserve of $27 million through fiscal conservatism, although doubters such as the *Herald* argued editorially that the money was a product of neglecting city services and employees.

Pradley's assertion that "(Evans) treats us like mechanics at the city garage" was shared by a number of police officers hoping union affiliation would instigate change.

The officers, according to comparisons of law enforcement salaries made by the newspapers, received inferior raises and frequently left for better pay with other departments after Brannon city government shouldered the cost of training recruits. Even administrative assistant Jenny Bowles was overheard telling the mayor he should consider higher salaries for the rank and file police officers.

The high turnover, however, corresponded with hiring experienced officers from other states eager to reside and work in Florida, accustomed to superior conditions, equipment, and pay, and savvy enough to finally vote in a police union at the Brannon Police Department.

The mayor was frustrated as the union ratcheted up demands, but figured plans for a new public safety complex would ease the discontent. He advocated construction of the "Town Center" containing a new city hall, police and fire departments on city-owned waterfront property downtown. Evans reasoned the city would not have to pay for the land, while enhancing an area that he was chastised for not energizing and developing more.

The drab property, part of a supposedly flood-prone, barren two-mile strip of marsh and scrub pines commonly occupied by the homeless, housed the dated municipal auditorium, which attracted an occasional concert, craft shows, tough-man contests and the mayor's annual "Feed the Homeless" Thanksgiving dinner.

What followed was "Decision Downtown," one of the most comprehensive public journalism initiatives in the annals of American newspapers. *Herald* coverage produced more than one article a day over four months, mostly disparaging the plan that enraged various constituencies. A host of influential developers wanted to purchase the site and adjacent land for the purpose of erecting hotels, restaurants, boating slips, and other amenities. The nearby arts community, residents, and merchants lodged concerns about parking and traffic, loud sirens from emergency response vehicles, and the prospect of felons defiling the area.

Content analysis of the coverage revealed twenty-one were editorials, one hundred twenty fit the news category, one appeared in the sports section of the newspaper, and five on the opinion page unveiling opinion polls, two of which solicited write-in votes about the complex with a third seeking public feedback by phone.

It was clear the editors at the *Herald*, among them Warren Posley and David Klemmert, had found a chink in the mayor's armor as he traversed his fifth four-year term in office. They were also waiting to see whether the city council would relent from its tendency to "rubber stamp" the mayor's agenda because of the potential fallout.

As city spokesman, Siebert realized the mayor was initially confident in the concept, mostly eschewing the opposition and blaming the *Herald*. The swarm of articles and public animosity accelerated in late July. In early September, a news article published interviews with citizens who rallied against the location in front of city hall. An editorial titled "We the People" claimed residents had sent a "powerful message" to the mayor and city council.

The mayor did not hold a town meeting until two weeks following the rally. "We had to call the meeting because the newspaper wasn't giving anything on our side of the issue," posited a council member. In a rare statement of appreciation, the *Herald* commended Evans editorially for doing so: "This is great news for citizens who felt locked out of the decision-making process."

The well-attended town meeting featured some ire and meaningful exchanges involving residents, the mayor, city council, and several department heads, but the headline in a news article the next day portrayed the bottom line: "Council doesn't budge." A second article reported that a female detractor of the proposed Town Center stood outside the meeting singing, "This land is your land, this land is my land, from the planetarium, to the playhouse theatre, from the auditorium" and so forth.

"Depending on who you talk to, there were eight hundred to a thousand people at the meeting," a local resident said. "We felt the council and mayor were flip and rude in answering questions. They just didn't get it. The meeting is really what got us interested in forming the PAC (Political Action Committee)."

The PAC, comprised largely of business people with the support of developers, urged residents to "take back" the city from its elected officials. It convened a steering committee to research different locations for the Town Center, making several failed recommendations to the council.

"I found myself in the unusual position of being on the same side of an issue as the newspaper," a member of the PAC said. "We put the committee together to review proposals for the sites, get better organized, raise money and get the information out."

Shortly thereafter, the city's twice-yearly newsletter written by Siebert offered residents an architectural rendering and overview detailing what the project would entail. It argued the Town Center would not only enliven downtown, but be cheaper, at just over $7 million, than other locations. It also polled city residents on whether they wanted their taxes to stay the same, or preferred watching them increase if another location were selected.

The newspaper editorially called the survey "loaded," claiming it posed a "leading question" to residents, who voted 149-15 against a tax hike.

In early December, the council announced it would not change the location of the complex, voting to proceed with the project sans the fire station, which would remain several blocks away.

"The newspaper and a few people downtown had waged a fear campaign about the fire station, worrying about sirens and ambulances, the narrow streets downtown," said the mayor. "It's funny, because county ambulances went down there all the time. We tried to appease them by taking out the fire station, but we knew they wouldn't be happy no matter what went down there."

A *Herald* editorial the next day claimed the council had made an "arrogant decision." It said the mayor and city council "will have their waterfront offices after all. In the end, public opinion about the wisdom of putting a public safety complex on the city's prime waterfront meant nothing to the council majority."

It concluded with an ominous warning: "One thing is for sure: There will be lots of people closely watching the mayor and all council members as the project moves forward."

While Garagolo registered the lone dissenting vote, less than one year later three of the four council members who favored the plan were handily defeated at the polls by challengers receiving editorial endorsements from the *Herald* and buttressed financially by the PAC.

"The public said they wanted a change in leadership," remarked the publisher. "I don't think the council members and the mayor really understood the scope of public concern about this issue."

Said a city department head: "The best way to describe the newspaper's role in writing about the project was vicious. I think they were looking for ways to get to the mayor."

"We couldn't counteract the newspaper's coverage of the public safety complex," asserted one of the vanquished council members. "It was overwhelming."

One incumbent was seeking his fifth term when he lost. The other two beaten incumbents had worked on various city boards for many years, and were vying for their second and third terms, respectively. They were also considered part of the mayor's political machine for many years.

According to a PAC member, "It's obvious the paper allocated a lot of space to articles and editorials. The newspaper's coverage of the issue played a role in the next year's elections, though I wouldn't call it a mandate. An editor of the paper did tell me he thought this issue was a defining moment in the future of this city."

The prestigious Pew Foundation for Public Journalism honored the *Herald's* "Destination Downtown" endeavors concerning the Town Center, something that did not impress the mayor when he called its office to say the organization's name was appropriate.

"I never witnessed that much coverage," groused the mayor. "They didn't write this much about World War II. With enough brainwashing and printing one side of the story, people will believe it."

What began as a public relations problem for the mayor, became a crisis. It is possible the political repercussions could have been mitigated with an earlier, more engaging response to community discontent despite the avalanche of adverse publicity.

The mayor would never occupy an office in the Town Center.

CHAPTER SIX

FROM MEDIA MADNESS TO MERCURIAL MAYOR

SEEING THE WRITING on the wall. Siebert departed the city four months before the election to assume a university professorship and consulting work with FEMA (Federal Emergency Management Agency) in Maryland, shedding the "PIO with a Ph.D." characterization. He had learned that Garagolo and Mary Barnes, a female socialite and PAC favorite who was eventually elected, would instigate a vote in January to eliminate his position and usurp more of the mayor's influence. Chief Thayer's interest in making him PIO for the police department, exclusively, was not sufficient motivation to stay.

Siebert and Walz had been instrumental in arranging the

Meet the Mayor morning AM radio call-in show featuring Evans, his platforms, and perspectives rarely advanced by the *Herald* and *Tribune*. In addition, an evening program on the same station, *The Heat is On*, was hosted by David O'Flannery, a stalwart advocate of the mayor. O'Flannery, viewed in some circles as a renegade loose cannon, attacked the editors of both newspapers incessantly.

Shortly before leaving, Siebert guest-hosted *Meet the Mayor* because Evans was unavailable. A *Tribune* columnist listened intently, realized there were few callers, and went on a lark the following morning in the newspaper, wondering how such an uncharismatic personality could possibly garner the attention of students in a college classroom. Siebert contacted the columnist, Toby Lyle, to chastise him for unwarranted hostility. The unrepentant Lyle said it was merely "tongue and cheek."

Knowing he was facing a daunting challenge with scant council support and a withering public relations team in his quest for re-election to a sixth term two years later, Evans rapidly extended the contracts of his department heads following the ouster of council members who voted for the Town Center. Joseph Hammond, a veteran *Tribune* columnist, wrote "Playing to lose: Evans' revenge game" excoriating the mayor and once again invoking the word bully.

The *Herald* applauded the election results as a chance for new horizons in the city, contradicting an allegedly inflexible, archaic regime. But few residents of the Brannon could have predicted the next chapter of the story announcing executive editor Warren Posley's campaign for mayor.

Sometimes officer promotions included reassignment, which certainly applied to Pradley when he became a patrol sergeant, vacating the detective bureau. His penchant for snooping around intrusively, in the minds of police administrators, was also incentive. Mayor Evans had told him on several occasions that he was disloyal to the police department and the city.

While driving his marked unit through a stately upper-class neighborhood one sunny afternoon, Pradley was waved over to the side of the road by a middle-aged woman who said her dog had gotten loose. She joined him in the vehicle, and they were able to locate the confused, missing animal standing in the middle of a nearby street. Within a couple of days, Mrs. Warren Posley had written Pradley's supervisor a thank you note for his courtesy.

Shortly thereafter, Pradley received a phone call from Warren Posley, who reminded him he was running for mayor and desired police backing. Pradley, a steward of the police union, agreed to meet the longtime *Herald* editor for breakfast a few miles south of the city limits.

Posley, who had unveiled his "Police for Posley" slogan, seemed strangely familiar with the police subterfuge Pradley discovered over the years as an investigator. He unsuccessfully prodded the detective for more details and Pradley, preserving investigative confidentiality, steered the conversation to the need for better pay, training, benefits, and an independent internal affairs unit, something Posley was apparently receptive to. In turn, Pradley was able to share the hopeful news with fellow union members inclined to support Posley's political aspirations.

Without an autonomous, certified IA unit of qualified police personnel, Pradley stated, "a police officer's suspected unprofessional behavior is investigated by his ranking supervisor and forwarded up the chain of command for review and comment. It is not uncommon for each reviewing supervisor to add his own take on the way the report should read, and how it should be resolved. The investigations are often slanted in favor of personal relationships, taking care of friends, and keeping officers employed."

The mayoral race was punctuated by mostly younger officers enamored of Posley's promises for reform and those largely content with the status quo. Some officers held Mayor Evans in contempt, while others, many of whom enjoyed privilege and promotion, found him relatable, a back-slapping former cop himself. The newspaper man could not match such personal connections or understanding of the law enforcement culture, but both camps recognized their livelihoods would likely be tied to the outcome of the election. Fierce, emotionally charged arguments were commonplace. The blue dividing line was also evident in candidates' forums.

While the Town Center was under construction, officers loathing Mayor Evans actually allowed K-9s making security rounds to relieve themselves where his office would supposedly be.

Hoping to bring them on board the Posley campaign train, Mary Barnes and a second new female council member, Karen Ruggiero, hosted parties for Brannon police officers. Some officers reciprocated, allowing the politicians to "ride along" with them on patrol. Sergeant Ricardo Hillyard, a key factor in the disgraceful Haverkamp saga, was among the revelers who found himself waffling between allegiance to the Evans regime and the possibility he could be defeated. In addition, Barnes eventually sparked the rehiring of Jim McManus, who had lost his job as an alleged Haverkamp accomplice years prior, and committed suicide not long after returning to the department.

Lieutenant Will Tovar, however, another memorable figure in the Haverkamp case and truly an Evans insider, never abandoned his devotion to the incumbent, at the same time being tapped by the incoming administration for his institutional knowledge.

With the endorsement of the *Heral*d and the *Tribune*, police union support, the largesse of developers and the PAC, and a depleted Evans following on the city council, Posley narrowly defeated his hated rival to become Brannon's mayor.

An early casualty of the fledgling hierarchy was Chief Thayer, forever associated with Evans and grappling for survival under Mayor Posley. Thayer retired soon after the election. He was replaced, with the new mayor's blessing, by Alvin Hobart, a former Sabella councilman and veteran undercover narcotics officer who ascended the ranks of the Sabella Police Department. The immensely likable, approachable Hobart had been one of Siebert's best sources when he was covering the police beat in Sabella.

Posley brought in *Herald* bowling writer Bo McCaffrey as a hybrid mayor's aide-city spokesman, enjoying pass key access to every division of the police department. McCaffrey, the self-described "troubleshooter," greeted those he encountered tersely: "I work for the mayor," spreading Posley's message at every opportunity.

Hobart, in concert with Posley, created a bona fide Internal Affairs unit headed up by Pradley, who received special training and credentialing for the role from esteemed law enforcement programs around the state. Citizens and city employees, including police officers, began lodging unsolicited complaints to the office located away from the public safety complex. Also prevalent were officers alleging neglect and mistreatment, past misconduct that went unchecked, and bending the ear of Chief Hobart to resolve departmental squabbles. The ability to address grievous concerns without political interference had improved, at least on the surface, while significant time was consumed defending the discretion and latitude of police officers who were serving the public faithfully.

In addition to McCaffrey's meddling, councilwomen Barnes and Ruggiero visited the office frequently to badger detectives about investigations pertaining to officers they had developed personal chemistry with. They were police "groupies" vicariously enjoying the adventure and drama the gun and badge symbolized, but not the IA scrutiny of their friends, one of whom was eventually fired for harboring pornography on his government laptop computer. All three of them touted executive oversight, demanding access to confidential information. They were rejected, enticing the wrath of Mayor Posley toward Chief Hobart and Pradley.

Egregious in the minds of Barnes and Ruggiero, was the

case of K-9 officer Jake Meyers, whom they, officers Ricardo Hillyard, Kedrick Danson, and Jim McManus socialized with exuberantly. Meyers landed on Pradley's radar when he could not produce any samples of cocaine, heroin or marijuana emanating from his dog's recognition training. They were supposed to be housed in a welded lock box inside the trunk of his cruiser.

When Pradley issued Meyers an immediate suspension pending further investigation, a political firestorm erupted.

Councilwoman Barnes was livid when she confronted Pradley in the IA office, slamming her hands on his desk. She questioned his integrity, claimed Meyers should have been warned in advance about the inspection, and accused him of "entrapment" before storming out.

Pradley forged ahead with the probe, discovering handcuffs, zip-ties, leashes, dog toys, and packages of condoms one evening in Meyers's locker.

Things really heated up, however, when a young woman anonymously called the IA unit to say an officer had asked her for late-night favors on a traffic stop.

Records indicated Meyers frequently pulled over female drivers on patrol, although most of the women contacted by IA for verification were unwilling to implicate the officer or get involved.

But one, a seventeen-year-old advised by her father to lodge a complaint, agreed to meet investigators for an interview. "Why is this asshole still working?" she asked upon observing his photograph displayed intentionally in the IA unit.

The teenager relayed how, after leaving her part-time job

at the mall, she observed flashing blue lights and stopped her car in the parking lot. The officer, she said, was at first cordial but then became agitated, asking whether she had a boyfriend, why she was driving alone at night, and indicating there would be no problems if she agreed to spend personal time in his vehicle.

Meyers was enraged when Pradley and a fellow investigator appeared at his house. His bewildered wife overheard much of the conversation, including a tepid explanation for why he carried condoms in his work bag, the contents of which were potential evidence toward possible sex abuse of a minor.

Pradley informed him that the missing drugs were a criminal matter, and the state would soon be reviewing the case.

The next day, Meyers phoned the police chief alleging internal affairs harassment and resigned from the force.

That same afternoon, councilwomen Barnes and Ruggiero descended upon Pradley in his office, saying he was overbearing, power hungry, and had a chip on his shoulder against upstanding officers in the department. They vowed to eject him from Internal Affairs with the approval of the mayor and police chief.

The stench of their perfume filled the air as they angrily departed.

At a pivotal juncture for the IA unit, one city employee voiced displeasure with a crusade by the mayor and Chief Hobart to tow abandoned cars from blighted areas of the city, apparently hoping to increase the value of properties owned by developers. Patrol officers were responsible for locating the vehicles and having the tow trucks dispatched.

The complainant also wanted to know what towing companies were involved, and why they could keep the vehicles as scrap metal sold for profit. Pradley quickly determined that only "Top Tier" towing company was being used, at the direction of Mayor Posley. More intriguing, albeit not overly surprising, was that Bo McCaffrey's brother-in-law owned the company that had not been sanctioned through the conventional bidding process.

Pradley learned from dispatchers that officers were mandated to make at least one "abandoned vehicle call" per shift, and that McCaffrey had echoed the mayor's edict to enlist only Top Tier towing. The dispatch supervisor advised that Chief Hobart had no comment when asked for verification.

After observing the towing monopoly first-hand in the ensuing weeks, Pradley interviewed an agitated McCaffrey at the IA office. He reminded Posley's toady that he must read him Miranda because his actions could comprise a first-degree misdemeanor for official misconduct as an agent of the mayor. McCaffrey unleashed a torrent of expletives and aborted the meeting. Within hours, Pradley was summoned to see Mayor Posley.

The mayor's secretary greeted Pradley with an icy stare. He noticed a large city map on the mayor's display table marked "to be developed" along the eastside waterfront inhabited by poor blacks and transient Hispanic workers, some of whom raised chickens and had dirt floors in their homes.

"What the fuck do you think you are doing?" bellowed the mayor, his face flushed with anger.

Pradley said he was upholding his oath to enforce the law, extrapolating the particulars of the investigation.

"There's no story here," huffed Posley, a journalistic retort he probably hoped for when the damning Schmitz pedophilia case erupted.

Private citizens could sometimes get away with lying and stealing, but not public servants, countered Pradley.

Posley accused Pradley of being "out of control," promising he would be removed from his position, which is precisely what occurred.

He went back on the road, also working as a school resource and training officer before retiring from the Brannon Police Department. From there, Pradley became the training coordinator at the Manson County Law Enforcement Academy, and was hired by the new Sabella-Brannon Airport police chief to assist in developing an agency affiliated with the Department of Homeland Security.

Hobart, who had been brokering raises for his officers but was tired of the politics roiling BPD and city government, became the Sand Key police chief after only one year at the helm. The IA office was disbanded by his successor per Posley's wishes.

Similar to the Evans regime, future investigations were funneled to front-line supervisors and reviewed by the chain of command, inviting the avarice of political alliances and personal friendships.

Years earlier, editorials reflecting the consensus of Posley and his colleagues at the *Herald* admonished Evans for "a far-fetched attempt to escape accountability," said he was "like some of the politicians of the past who governed more dictatorially than is acceptable today," and added, "The principle has to do with openness. Trust. Candor. The principle is critical to the success of any politician."

The greatest irony, or perhaps hypocrisy, was that Posley's election closely coincided with completion of the Town Center on city-owned property he had contested vociferously as executive editor when the *Herald* lamented that the mayor and council "will have their waterfront offices after all."

EPILOGUE

I BELIEVE BEING a police officer is the most honorable job in the world. As police officers, we have the chance to affect our lives and communities every day. People rely on us to provide protection and emergency services.

They expect us to know what to do in critical situations. For the most part, people believe in us. They expect us to make the right decisions. They always expect us to do the right thing.

Most of the decisions you will make as a police officer won't be a choice between right and wrong. Those are easy decisions. The hard decisions you will be faced with are those which deal between right and right. You will be faced with choosing the "best" right.

You should prepare to make those decisions, because the time is very near when you will be faced with one. Understand that the things most important to you—family, spouse, and children, will be greatly affected by your decisions. When you arrive at a decision, you will want to protect the things you value most. If you can openly and honestly explain your decisions to those you treasure, you are making honest decisions.

In 1994, a group of midshipmen at the United States Naval Academy were caught cheating on their exams. The Academy has an honor code that each midshipman swears to uphold. Like police officers, the integrity of a Naval officer is considered to be his greatest asset.

When confronted with the prospect of turning each other in for cheating, many maintained a "Code of Silence." Those midshipmen were thrown out of the corps and dishonorably discharged from the service.

In his remarks to them, Marine Colonel Michael W. Hagee said: "The loyalty that would cause an individual to jump on a hand grenade to save other lives is good. But to venerate loyalty at all costs, as did those students who refused to turn in their classmates for cheating, ignored a more important truth: Honesty."

Could you feel good about explaining to your child that it's okay to cheat a little as long as you don't get caught? Where do you draw the line?

When making decisions, review your list of values. Consider the other people and things that are affected by your decision: your family, your spouse, your children, your integrity. Make your off-duty decisions the same way you make your on-duty decisions...based on your values, and at the end of the day you will be satisfied with yourself.

Pay attention to what goes on around you. Conduct yourself accordingly. There is a syndrome known as the boiling frog syndrome. As you know, frogs are cold-blooded; their body temperature will slowly adjust to the temperature surrounding it. If you put a frog in a pan of water and place it on the stove top, heating the water, the frog's body will slowly match that of the water around it. The water temperature and the frog's body temperature will both increase at the same time. Imagine what happens to the frog once the water around it begins to boil.

Unhealthy situations don't happen overnight; they slowly creep up on you. You are about to become a frog in a large pan of heated water. Pay attention to what is happening around you and protect yourself—don't' be afraid to stand up for what you believe in, even if you are the only one willing to do so.

Confucius once said, "When the superior man deals with the world he is not for or against anything. He does what is right."

Everything gets updated. Radios, cars, weapons, uniforms—they are all continually replaced with newer, better models. What we need is something that would make better people also. We must think about how we can model ourselves to become better from the inside out.

From the first time you polish your new badge, I want you to think about the badge on the inside, deep within yourself. That badge is the one that only you can see, the one that will stay with you long after you leave law enforcement. The badge that you wear inside will always reflect your decisions and real values. How shiny is that badge? It will reflect your true character.

What things will help you keep your inner badge shiny?

Trustworthiness: the commitment to truth as well as avoidance of cheating and trickery.

Respect: treat everyone and everything with respect.

Responsibility: be accountable for your decisions, don't shift blame, and lead by example.

Justice and fairness: show equity and consistency in all you do.

Caring: show concern for others, always considering how your decision will influence their lives.

Civic virtue and citizenship: develop a social consciousness beyond your own self-interest.

These examples of character will provide you with an anchor to measure your behavior.

Were there any that you disagreed with?

Any that you did not want associated with your name?

There is no checklist for bad things we should not do; there is only the belief that we have the ability to do things right. As police officers, we are expected to do the right thing, on and off duty. If you want to be a police officer in a free society, you must be willing to accept public scrutiny. After all, a police officer's sworn testimony can take away the rights of a citizen.

With that being the case, how important is a police officer's integrity to the public?

Should the public demand that their police officers be honest in everything they do or in just some of the things they do?

Should a police officer be held to a higher standard?

When the newspaper reports on an officer's alleged misconduct, should we talk to the paper about "hounding the police," or talk to the officer about public trust?

If an on-duty officer catches an off-duty officer in a traffic violation, and lets him go without a ticket, even though he would have issued a ticket to a citizen, is that officer upholding the public trust?

How do you explain his act of "professional courtesy" to the general public?

Would you want to have to explain that concept to anyone?

How would you explain it to your child?

The term "professional courtesy," as used by some law enforcement officers, is simply "situational ethics." Donald Soderquist, of John Brown University, defines situational ethics as being the result of "inconsistent standards." It suggests that it is okay to lie…sometimes…and it's okay to cheat…for some people.

In 1989, a researcher named Delattre made the following statement:

> "Society expects police officers as public servants and upholders of the law, to conduct themselves with more honor and restraints than most other citizens. Neither the police nor the public should misconstrue this standard as unfair: it is not a double standard. Persons accepting positions of public trust take on new obligations, which they may decline to accept if they do not wish to abide by a higher standard."

Policing in a democratic society is the most difficult police work in the world. Police officers visibly represent the government in everything they do, one or off duty. The public trust is threatened whenever an officer involves himself in any sort of misconduct. Delattre defined integrity as "keeping your promises."

What promises has a sworn police officer made to his community?

When you are hired by an agency, and are taking your oath, listen carefully to the words you are saying. Then ask yourself, what acts are you willing to overlook as an officer who is sworn to uphold the law? How good must you be? Should you as a police officer be held to a higher standard? No matter what you believe, rest assured, you will be held to a higher standard.

During the American Revolution many people had to make hard decisions that affected many other people. Men like Washington, Paine, Jefferson and Madison were faced with terrible odds. They were outgunned and outmanned at every turn. Their competition was the King of England.

In making their decisions, they demonstrated a high degree of determination and passion. They demonstrated their inner values. They all faced the very real possibility of being hanged by the King, but they all held true to their inner beliefs. These men kept in constant written contact with each other during their struggle, each urging the other to "do the right thing."

Here are some of the isolated comments these inspirational leaders wrote to each other that are very applicable to police officers today:

> Hope for the best, but prepare for the worst.
>
> Endeavor to make fitness of character a primary object.
>
> Spit not into the fire.
>
> Analyze your situation with a childlike point of view, and no biases.
>
> Rally every member of the organization to a common cause.

Be a frequent reader of the controversial literature of the day.

Liston, then speak; follow, then lead.

Work by day, think by night.

Try to remain optimistic even when you are in an extremely dangerous situation.

To form an idea, you must be on the spot.

When outnumbered, keep at a distance; neither fight, nor run away.

March when the competition is sleeping.

Never give up hope.

Fight for your honor when it is attacked.

Keep your sense of humor, even during the worst moments of crisis.

Be smart enough to realize you can't do it all yourself.

Encourage others to lead.

Pay attention and establish trust.

Do not act without asking; take time to verify key information.

Never give up, never give in.

Have the courage to seize your one moment in time.

Those who lead must be willing to take chances.

Develop future leaders.

Pass the torch to the next generation…

…and remember that one inspiring communication can turn the tide.

—Patrick J. Proudler
Commencement keynote speaker
Manson County Law Enforcement Academy

I WANT TO thank Pat for his inspirational statement. I have always remembered his assertion that "being a cop is only easy in a police state." It has been my pleasure to work with him, both in law enforcement and on this project concerning police, politics, and the press. We believe the theme is unique and highly relevant today. In closing, I ask readers to consider whether social media might have altered our story, or contemporary ones with similar elements. For example, we can imagine the lawless officers and their friends in the first chapter posting incriminating messages and photographs of stolen bounty to the delight of investigators. Editorials, letters to the editor and traditional commercial media crossfire, while still extremely cogent, are now players in the dizzying swirl of cyberspace opinions, rumors, and innuendo, with serious repercussions for persuasion and public information. The cop narrative is crafted with cameras and personal devices, a new brand of investigative documentation capable of boosting and ruining careers. Policing is heavily scrutinized by citizens wielding cell phones. The perpetrator in the sex crimes case would have been likely to exploit his victims through social media. Think of the Internet bloodletting over the public safety complex. And the possibility that the incumbent mayor, lacking the obvious publicity advantages of the newspaper editor, could have balanced the pendulum enough with social media to win another term.

—Haven P. Simmons

ABOUT THE AUTHORS

HAVEN P. SIMMONS, Ph.D. worked in and around the media nearly fifteen years for two daily newspapers, two ABC television affiliates, and as a city government spokesman. He has taught media relations-public information in mock disaster courses at the Federal Emergency Management Agency (FEMA) for more than two decades. Dr. Simmons also teaches communication at the National Fire Academy, and was an observer-controller for NERRTC (National Emergency Response and Recovery Training Center) in Texas. He retired as a communication professor in Maryland. Dr. Simmons holds Ph.D. and M.A. degrees from the University of Iowa. His dissertation and assorted publications studied the relationship of the media and law enforcement.

VETERAN LAW ENFORCEMENT officer Patrick J. Proudler spent seventeen years in a municipal police department working as a patrolman, detective, and internal affairs investigator, reaching the rank of lieutenant. He was a public service and training coordinator for a county law enforcement academy and school district. He served as a corporal and accreditation manager with an airport authority police department under the Department of

Homeland Security (DHS). Mr. Proudler was honorably discharged after four years in the U.S. Navy. He also worked as a corrections officer. Mr. Proudler holds an A.A. degree from Pennsylvania State University, in addition to extensive law enforcement certification from state and national police academies. He is also the author of *Cops and Robbers,* to be published in early 2021.

ACKNOWLEDGMENTS

AS A YOUNG man escaping from cold weather Iowa to Florida in a Chevy with Fred Flintstone floorboards, I had no idea how many twists and turns there would be on my career highway that mercifully never succumbed to boredom or drudgery. I certainly met many interesting, talented and gracious people, some of whom are named in these acknowledgments while others must remain anonymous.

I am grateful to veteran sports journalists Gus Schrader and Jack Ogden, who hired me as a fourteen-year-old at our home town newspaper in Cedar Rapids. Also to Jim Gray at the Gate City in Keokuk, where I was sports editor, a position that ignited our friendship lasting two decades. Hey, Mark Twain got his start at the same publication, my modest claim to fame. Thank goodness for the two reporters at the Sabella paper showing me the ropes covering the cop beat and the layout editor, soon to become one of my best friends as I navigated the graduate school years and beyond.

Thank you to the many trusted Sabella law enforcement sources and friends, including the chief detective who instigated my new job at the local ABC affiliate. My boss at the station also deserves thanks for assigning countless Manson County news stories and later naming me sports director. The mayor, the sheriff, other officials, my closest PIO comrade, myriad contacts, law enforcement officers, and friends were fantastic in Manson County and Brannon, the impetus and setting for this case study. I so much appreciate the mayor hiring me as PIO, a role that fueled many rewarding opportunities and experiences, including my marriage.

Thanks to Al Fluman, I have been a media-public information instructor at the Federal Emergency Management Agency (FEMA) twenty-three years. Thank you, as well, to studio technicians Jim Blazes and Bill Hertel for facilitating those essential newscasts and press conferences. Thank you to Russ Johnson, my good friend during graduate studies at the the University of Iowa, the most courageous person I know against overwhelming odds. Our weekly conversations about career and the game of life have been comforting.

Suffice to say, my advanced degrees, decades of teaching many enjoyable communication students at Salisbury University in Maryland, and consulting would not have been possible without professor, mentor, and dear friend Al Talbott at the UI. He was a scholar who understood the relevance of real-world pedigree and application in the classroom, fearlessly receptive to a variety of doctoral dissertation topics.

Most of all, I cherish the love and devotion of my wife, Luvy, undoubtedly the career highlight since we met working together for Brannon city government.

—Haven Simmons

www.copworldpress.com

www.ingramcontent.com/pod-product-compliance
Lightning Source LLC
Chambersburg PA
CBHW050356280326
41933CB00010BA/1491
* 9 7 8 1 9 4 6 7 5 4 1 5 8 *